Cambridge English

OFFICIAL

FUN for Movers

T0373862

Student's Book
Fourth edition

Anne Robinson
Karen Saxby

Cambridge University Press
www.cambridge.org/elt

Cambridge Assessment English
www.cambridgeenglish.org

Information on this title: www.cambridge.org/9781316631959

© Cambridge University Press & Assessment 2016

First published 2006
Second edition 2010
Third edition 2015
Fourth edition 2016

40 39 38

Printed in Dubai by Oriental Press

A catalogue record for this publication is available from the British Library

ISBN 978-1-316-61753-3 Student's Book with online activities with audio and Home Fun booklet
ISBN 978-1-316-63195-9 Student's Book with online activities with audio
ISBN 978-1-316-61755-7 Teacher's Book with downloadable audio
ISBN 978-1-108-72815-7 Presentation Plus

The authors and publishers would like to thank the ELT professionals who commented on the material at different stages of its development.

The authors are grateful to: Niki Donnelly of Cambridge University Press.

Anne Robinson would like to give special thanks to Adam Evans and her parents Margaret and Jim and to many, many teachers and students who have inspired her along the way. Special thanks to Cristina and Victoria for their help, patience and enthusiasm. And in memory of her brother Dave.

Karen Saxby would like to give special thanks to everyone she has worked with at Cambridge Assessment since the birth of YLE! She would particularly like to mention Frances, Felicity and Ann Kelly. She would also like to acknowledge the enthusiasm of all the teachers she has met through her work in this field. And lastly, Karen would like to say a big thank you to her sons, Tom and William, for bringing constant FUN and creative thinking to her life and work.

Freelance editorial services by Angela Janes

Design and typeset by Wild Apple Design.

Cover design by Chris Saunders (Astound).

Sound recordings by dsound Recording Studios, London

The authors and publishers acknowledge the following sources of copyright material and are grateful for the permissions granted. While every effort has been made, it has not always been possible to identify the sources of all the material used, or to trace all copyright holders. If any omissions are brought to our notice, we will be happy to include the appropriate acknowledgements on reprinting and in the next update to the digital edition, as applicable.

The authors and publishers are grateful to the following illustrators:

T = Top, B = Below, L = Left, R = Right, C = Centre, B/G = Background

The authors and publishers are grateful to the following illustrators:

Laetitia Aynié (Sylvie Poggio Artists Agency) pp. 6 (T), 7 (BL), 17 (C), 19, 29 (T), 30 (BL), 31 (B), 33 (T), 39 (T), 48, 58 (B), 62 (C), 63 (T), 67 (B), 77 (B), 81 (C), 82 (T), 90 (T), 92, 100 (T); Johanna A Boccardo (Sylvie Poggio Artists Agency) pp. 36 (B), 52, 53 (CR), 68 (TR); Nina de Polonia (Advocate Art) pp. 11 (T), 18 (C), 21 (C), 24 (TL), 27 (B), 40, 60 (B), 69 (C), 104; Bridget Dowty (Graham-Cameron Illustration) pp. 23 (CL), 26 (T), 39 (B), 74 (T); Andy Elkerton (Sylvie Poggio Artists Agency) pp. 8 (T), 9 (T), 21 (B), 28 (C), 51 (T), 58 (T), 73 (T), 89 (B), 109, 110; Chris Embleton-Hall (Advocate Art) pp. 28 (T), 46 (T); Brett Hudson (Graham-Cameron Illustration) pp. 29 (BR), 31 (C), 38 (1, 2, 5, 6, 8) (B) , 55, 61 (C), 70 (B), 71, 73 (C, T), 76 (T), 80 (T), 83 (B), 94 (T); Nigel Kitching (Sylvie Poggio Artists Agency) pp. 8 (C), 12, 17 (T), 42, 43, 62 (T), 64, 106 (BR), 108; Andrew Painter (Sylvie Poggio Artists Agency) pp. 10 (C), 11 (B), 15 (C), 25 (T), 35, 37 (T), 48 (B), 50 (C), 51 (B), 53 (BR), 63 (B), 66 (C), 68 (B), 78, 79 (T), 84, 85, 88 (B), 93 (B), 98 (TR), 102 (B), 103 (B), 112 (B), 114 (T), 115; Jamie Pogue (The Bright Agency) pp. 9 (B), 20, 24 (B), 36 (B, T), 45, 47, 59 (C), 60 (T), 61 (BR), 111, 112 (T); Andrejs Ricci (The Organisation) pp. 6 (B), 13, 16 (B), 23 (BR), 32 (T), 34, 38 (3, 4, 7), 41 (BR), 53 (T), 76 (B), 77 (T), 79 (B), 83 (T), 88 (T), 97, 101, 103 (T); Anthony Rule pp. 5, 7 (BR), 11 (BC), 18 (TR), 25 (B), 28 (TR), 31 (BR), 33 (BR), 36 (TR), 37 (BR), 44 (TR), 49 (CR), 50 (TR), 59 (TR), 66 (TR), 69 (BR), 74 (TR), 79 (BR), 85 (BR), 87 (BR), 88 (TR), 96 (TR), 104 (T); Pip Sampson pp. 15 (T), 18 (BR), 22, 23 (CR), 30 (T), 31 (T), 38 (T), 56, 57, 62 (B), 72, 73 (B), 82 (B), 90 (B), 94 (B), 95, 96 (C), 102 (TR), 106 (TR), 107; Melanie Sharp (Sylvie Poggio Artists Agency) pp. 10 (TR), 16 (T), 17 (B), 41 (T), 54, 67 (T), 81 (B), 86, 98 (C), 99, 105, 113, 114; Emily Skinner p. 93 (T); Jo Taylor (Sylvie Poggio Artists Agency) pp. 25, 74 (B), 75, 89 (T), 100 (BR); Matt Ward @ Beehive pp. 62 (B), 96, 101; Sarah Wimperis (Graham-Cameron Illustration) pp. 46 (BL), 91; Sue Woollatt pp. 14, 26 (B), 27 (T), 44 (C), 70 (T), 80, 87.

Contents

1 Watch us! We're moving!

A ▶ Listen and draw lines.

May   Eva   Tom   Sue   Dan

Jane   Pat   Jack   Jill   Sam

....

B Read and write names.

Watch us! We're moving!

....Jack.....'s good at jumping. He's really great!

And look! ....'s hopping on square number 8!

............'s roller skating! She's going round and round.

And watch .... skipping in our new playground.

............'s good at dancing! One, two, three.

And there's .... He's funny! He's climbing our tree!

............'s very good at running. He runs all day!

But .... likes walking (and talking) with her best friend, ...

Jump, hop, skate, skip,

dance, climb or run.

We all love moving and having lots of fun!

C Listen and draw four things in picture A.

D Find the letters to spell the missing moving word!

_ _ _ _ b _ _ _ _

E Look and read and write.

Examples   The boy with the radio is wearing ...... *a yellow T-shirt* ....
Which number is the girl's foot on now?   .... *8* ....

Complete the sentences. Write 1, 2, 3, 4 or 5 words.

1   The boy in the orange jacket is ....
2   At the front of the picture you can see ....

Answer the questions. Write 1, 2, 3, 4 or 5 words.

3   One girl is skipping. What colour are her trousers?   ....
4   What's the girl with the red balloon doing?   ....

Now write one sentence about the picture.

5   ....

F About you! Say and write answers.

Who do you play with in your playground?   I play with ....
Is your playground big or small?   It's ....
What are you good at?   I'm good at ....

Tell me about your friend.

What's your friend's name?   My friend's name is ....
How old is your friend?   My friend is ....
What's your friend good at?   ....

2 Animals, animals ...

A Say then write the animals.

1	2	3	4 ....
5	6	7	8 ....
9	10	11	12 ....
13	14	15	

B Which parts of a crocodile can you see in pictures 1–4?

its .... its .... its .... its .... and its ....

C How much do you know about crocodiles? Write yes or no.

1 Do crocodiles only live in rivers?   ....
2 Do crocodiles open their eyes when they are swimming?   ....
3 Can crocodiles swim and walk?   ....
4 Do crocodiles have lots of teeth?   ....
5 Do crocodiles eat birds?   ....
6 Is it safe to go swimming with a crocodile?   ....
7 Is a baby crocodile inside its egg for 20 weeks?   ....

Are your answers right? Read about crocodiles on page 106.

D Read and write the animal names.

Example	It has a tail and it likes catching mice. It sounds like 'hat'.	*cat*
1	It's small, black and yellow and it can fly. It sounds like 'me'.	....
2	It's always hungry and it has a little beard. It sounds like 'boat'.	....
3	It's very small and it eats cheese. It sounds like 'house'.	....
4	It's green and it jumps very well. It sounds like 'dog'.	....
5	It eats grass. It sounds like 'now'.	....
6	It sings and sometimes lives in a cage. It sounds like 'word'.	....
7	It lives in the sea. I'm frightened of it! It sounds like 'park'.	....
8	It has no legs and makes a noise like 'sssss'. It sounds like 'cake'.	....
9	It's really big and it swims in the sea. It sounds like 'tail'.	....
10	It flies at night. It sounds like 'Pat'.	....

E ▶ Listen and write.

Peter's day at the zoo

Example	Name of zoo:	..........*World*.......... Zoo
1	Who with:	....
2	Can see:	.... monkeys
3	Favourite animals:	....
4	Can ride on:	a ....
5	Wants to buy:	a ....

F Funtime Now play the game! It sounds like ... .

3 Fun at the farm

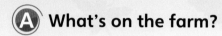

A What's on the farm?

a cloud

a field

a truck

a roof

a chicken

a rabbit

a duck

a kitten

a tractor

B Read and then complete the sentences. Write one word.

> **Let's go to Mrs Plant's farm!**
> On Saturday afternoons, ... and his sister, ... , go to help Mrs Plant on her farm. They carry potatoes and feed all the different animals. The children ride there on their bikes because it is near their home. Mrs Plant has two new animals on the farm now! She's got a kitten called Sunny and a puppy called Sausage! They're both really sweet.

1 The children go to the farm every ...Saturday... afternoon.
2 Mrs .... lives on the farm.
3 The children .... Mrs Plant's potatoes for her.
4 At the farm, the kids give the .... their food.
5 The children ride their .... to the farm.
6 Mrs Plant's kitten is called ....
7 The pets on the farm are very ....

C ▶ Listen and colour.

D Say which picture is different and why.

1

2

3

4

E Which animals live in these places? Write their names.

Which three animals are you frightened of? ....
....

Which are your three favourite animals? ....
....

Which animal would you like to be?
I'd like to be a ....!

F Sounding the same!

there

they're

their

G Do the animal project!

PROJECT

11

4 Your hair looks great!

A Write the answers to the questions.

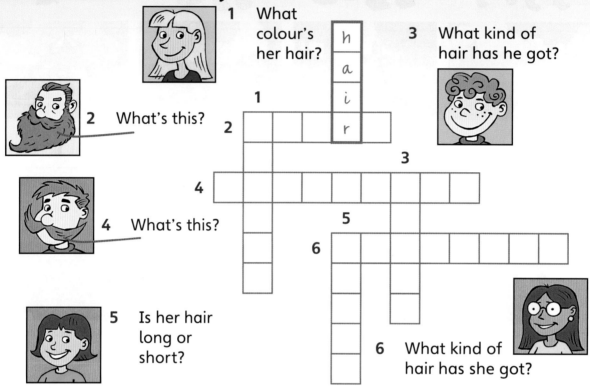

1 What colour's her hair?

2 What's this?

3 What kind of hair has he got?

4 What's this?

5 Is her hair long or short?

6 What kind of hair has she got?

B Talk about your hair.

| I've got | long | straight | blonde fair red brown | hair. |
| I have | *short* | | black grey/gray white | |

C ▶ Listen and tick (✔) the box.

1 Which girl is Kim?

A ☐   B ☐   C ☐

2 Which man is Mr Scarf?

A ☐   B ☐   C ☐

3 Which person is Jim's cousin?

A ☐   B ☐   C ☐

4 Which boy is Paul's friend?

A ☐   B ☐   C ☐

D Read about Hugo. Write 1, 2 or 3 words to complete the sentences.

Change Hugo's face for the film.

Hugo Top is really famous because he's a film star. The name of his seventh film is *What's that noise?* Hugo is making it now. In this film, his body and face look very different. Hugo is an alien!

Before filming, Hugo puts on his orange alien suit and then sits down in front of a big mirror. Then Alice starts changing his face. First, she paints it green. Then someone paints black lines on his face and changes the colour of his eyes.

A third person, called Matt, adds a moustache and beard to Hugo's face and a fourth person changes his short, straight blonde hair to long, curly purple hair!

Then Hugo can start filming. 'Your face looks really ugly and scary now!' everyone says. Hugo looks in the mirror again and laughs. 'Well, I think I look really cool!' he says, 'Thank you!'

Examples   Hugo Top is a ....*famous*........ film star.
His seventh film is called ....*What's that noise?*....

1   In Hugo's new film, his .... and body look very different.
2   Hugo sits down in front of a .... in his orange clothes.
3   A woman makes Hugo's face green. Her name is ....
4   Another person paints some .... on his face, too.
5   Matt puts two things on Hugo's face – a ....
6   Hugo has to have ...., curly and purple hair in this film.
7   Everyone thinks Hugo's face looks very ....!

E Funtime Play the game! Find the person.

F She looks surprised!

5 The woman in the red dress

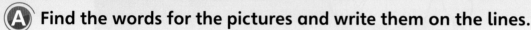

A Find the words for the pictures and write them on the lines.

1

.... scarf ....

s	c	a	r	f	g	s	s	c
w	o	s	s	b	l	k	h	a
e	a	h	o	o	a	i	o	p
a	t	i	c	o	s	r	r	d
t	w	r	k	t	s	t	t	r
e	b	t	s	s	e	p	s	e
r	t	r	o	u	s	e	r	s
s	w	i	m	s	u	i	t	s

8

....

7

....

2

....

3

....

4

....

5

....

6

....

B Find the words in the box for five more things people wear.

C Choose the correct words from A or B. Write them on the lines.

1 In cold weather, you can wear this round your neck. a .... scarf ....
2 This is like a very long jacket which you can wear outside. a ....
3 You can wear these on your feet inside your shoes. ....
4 A girl can wear this when she wants to go in the sea. a ....
5 A pair of these can help some people to read a book. ....

D Say the words.

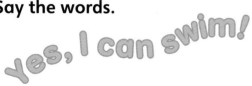

No, I can't fly!

E Write the words from A and B in the table.

top half	bottom half	top and bottom half
scarf	a pair of socks	coat

F ▶ Listen and draw lines.

Anna   Fred   Mark   Peter

Lucy   Jane   Tom

G Look and read and write.

Examples   The baby is sitting under a .... *tree* ....
            What's the girl in the short skirt holding?   .... *an ice cream* ....

Complete the sentences. Write 1, 2, 3, 4 or 5 words.

1   The pink monster is trying to catch ....

2   The old man has got a   ....

Answer the questions. Write 1, 2, 3, 4 or 5 words.

3   The mother is sitting on a seat. What colour is it?   ....

4   Two children are on bikes. What have they got on their heads? ....

Now write two sentences about the picture.

5   ....

6   ....

15

6 My neck, my shoulders

(A) How many?

hands	26
eyes	....
legs	....
ears	....
backs	....
mouths	....
wings	....

(B) Longer than, shorter than?
Cross out the wrong word.

The monsters' legs are *longer / shorter* than the children's legs.

The children's hair is *longer / shorter* than the monster's hair.

The monsters' mouths are *bigger / smaller* than the children's mouths.

The children's heads are *bigger / smaller* than the monsters' heads.

The man is *shorter / taller* and *younger / older* than everyone!

(C) My neck, my shoulders and my stomach!

Listen and point.

my neck

my shoulder

my stomach

D **Find the correct words and write them on the lines.**

Example   This is between your eyes and your mouth. .... *nose* ....

1   After your dinner, your food is inside this. ....

2   This is hair on a man's face. It's under his mouth. ....

3   You stand on these. They are at the end of your legs. ....

4   These are white and you have lots in your mouth. ....

5   You have two of these and you listen with them. ....

6   This is under your head and above your shoulders. ....

searsoteethlnosehfeeteneckrstomachubeardd

The mystery word is ....

E **Put the balls in the correct net!**

1 The monsters' arms are very short.

2 One of the monsters is holding a cup.

3 There's a flower on one monster's stomach.

4 The robot that's outside the house is laughing.

5 You can see a monster on the round roof.

6 The monster next to the door is wearing a pair of shoes.

F **The monsters go home to the moon! Listen and colour.**

G **Funtime** **Play the game! Answer with your body.**

7 What's the weather like?

A Draw the missing pictures.

a coat	clouds	the wind	a kangaroo
rain	bats	a scarf	the moon

B Choose the correct words and write them on the lines.

Example   This is longer than a jacket and you wear it outside. ....*a coat*........

1   You can see this and the stars above you at night. ....

2   These only fly at night and some people are afraid of them. ....

3   When you walk in this weather, your clothes get wet! ....

4   This animal can hop and it lives in a hot, sunny, country. ....

5   It's a good idea to wear this round your neck on colder days. ....

6   These are white or grey and sometimes snow falls from them. ....

C ▶ Charlie and Lily's favourite weather.

wind   sunny   windy   raining   fly   bike   ride   kite

1   Charlie likes .... weather because when it is ....
     he can't .... his .... to school.

2   Lily is happy when it is .... because she needs
     the .... to .... her ....

D Vicky's painting class. Complete the first part of the story.

It's a _ _ _ _ _ _ _ day at Vicky's _ _ _ _ _ _ _ .
Vicky's in her painting _ _ _ _ _ _ .
She's thinking, 'What can I _ _ _ _ _ ?'

Vicky

Now you tell the story.

Where's Vicky now?
What's she thinking about?
Has she got any ideas?

Where's Vicky now?
What's she looking at?
Has she got an idea now?

Where's Vicky now?
What's in her painting?
Who's saying, 'Well done!'

E Match sentences and story pictures. Write 1, 2, 3 or 4.

1   Wow! Look at that rainbow in the sky! It's fantastic! picture ③

2   That's a really pretty picture, Vicky! picture ◯

3   My friend's got a great idea but I haven't. picture ◯

4   I can't find any cool pictures in this library or on this website. Oh dear! picture ◯

F ▶ Draw the weather.
What's it like?
Is it hot or cold?
Is it sunny or windy or cloudy?
Is it raining or snowing?
Can you see a rainbow?

8 The hottest and coldest places

A Find sentence pairs about different kinds of weather.

I'm white.

I make the leaves fall from trees.

I can change things from dry to wet!

You only see me when the sun's behind you!

I come from grey clouds.

I come out when you go to bed.

Look carefully to see my seven colours.

When you see me, you can see stars, too.

You want me when you go sailing!

I only fall on really, really cold days.

I'm hot, big and round.

No, you can't see me at night!

B Listen and write and say!

Is it right to fly a kite at night?

C Complete the sentences with words from the box.

1

2

3

4

5

6

1 There's lots of ice in Antarctica. It's the ....coldest.......... place in the world.

2 The .... town is in India. It rains there a lot!

3 Africa is the .... part of the world.

4 The .... place is Antarctica, too. The wind there is really strong!

5 In Arizona, it's always dry and sunny! It's the .... place the USA.

driest
coldest
sunniest
wettest
windiest
hottest

20

D **Choose words to complete the weather sentences.**

It is
It was

windy
cloudy
sunny
hot
cold

today.
yesterday.

It
It

is raining
is snowing
rained
snowed

today.
yesterday.

E **Choose the correct words and write them on the lines.**

Animals in cold parts of the world

We don't see many animals in the coldest parts of the world, but polar bears, which are white, ...*live*........ in really cold places.

lived	live	living

Example

1 Brown bears .... when the weather is very cold.

| 1 | sleep | sleeping | sleeps |

2 .... don't wake up or eat any food.

| 2 | It | They | We |

3 When the weather starts getting cold, some birds fly .... hotter countries, but penguins are very happy in the snow!

| 3 | by | to | at |

4 Snowshoe rabbits are really clever! .... the weather's very cold and

| 4 | When | Why | Which |

5 there's snow on the ground, ... animal's fur changes from brown to white!

| 5 | those | all | this |

F **Which are the tallest, strongest and cleverest animals?**

G **Let's write funny sentences!**

9 Me and my family

A Who are they? Listen and draw lines.

Hugo and Zoe Rice

Matt and Alice Page

Sam and Julia Rice

Jane (13)   Sue (11)   Ben (12)   Peter (5)

B Read about Jane. Write the family words on the lines.

My sister, Sue, and I love everyone in our family! Our parents are great! (1) ....Dad....'s
name is Matt. Our (2) ....'s called Alice. We've got a really pretty (3) ....,
too. She's called Julia and our (4) ....'s name is Sam. He's very tall! We've got
two (5) .... They're both boys and their names are Ben and Peter.
Our (6) ....' names are Hugo and Zoe. We like going to see them a lot!
They're happy because they've got two granddaughters and two grandsons now, Ben,
Peter, Sue and me!

C Answer questions about the people in your family.

		My answers	My friend's answers
1	Who's the oldest?	....	....
2	Who's the youngest?	....	....
3	Who's the loudest?	....	....
4	Who's the quietest?	....	....
5	Who's the cleverest?	....	....
6	Who's the busiest?	....	....
7	Who's the prettiest?	....	....
8	Who's the naughtiest?	....	....
9	Who's the coolest?	....	....
10	Who's the silliest?	....	....

D Write 1, 2 or 3 words to complete the sentences about the story.

On holiday at the farm

Hello! My name's Ben. I live in the town centre with my parents and my brother, Peter. Peter's younger than me. He's five and I'm twelve. Last Saturday, Dad took us all to our grandparents' farm in his car. Grandma and Grandpa live on a farm that's near the sea. We love going there.

Examples   Ben and Peter's home is in <u>the town centre</u> .
........................<u>Ben</u>........................ is twelve years old.

1   The children went to their grandparents' farm by the sea last ....
2   Ben, his brother and father travelled by ....

There's always something exciting to go and see at their farm. On Sunday, my brother asked, 'Can we go and see the horses, Grandpa?' 'Yes!' Grandpa said. 'And I can show you our two new baby horses! They're only one week old. I'd like you to choose names for them!' Grandpa added. 'Good idea!' Grandma said.

3   The children went to see the two .... on Sunday.
4   Grandpa asked the boys to choose the baby horses' ....

Peter and I laughed when we saw the baby horses! They had pretty brown eyes and made funny noises when we said, 'Your new names are Cloudy and Star!' On Monday, we both rode Mr Jim, Grandpa's oldest horse, around the biggest field. Peter and I really loved that holiday. It was fantastic.

5   The boys called the two baby horses ....
6   The boys rode Mr Jim around their grandfather's ....
7   Ben and his brother enjoyed .... a lot!

E Can you hear the sound 'Zzzzzzzz'?

boys   names   who's   always
answers   his   noises   he's   horses
busiest   legs   Thursday   eyes   ours

10 People in our street

A Write ten words to put in the gaps. You choose!

Hi! I live in (1) .... Street. There are only about
(2) .... houses and flats in our street.

I don't know everyone but we're friends with the Fish family.
They live in a huge (3) .... house. It's got lots of
windows and a funny (4) .... roof. Mr Fish is a
sports teacher and he likes cooking (5) .... on his
balcony! Mrs Fish gives dancing and music lessons. She can
play the (6) .... really well. She can make really great
chocolate (7) .... too!

Mr and Mrs Fish have got a son who's called (8) ....
He's got a pet (9) ....! I really like playing
(10) .... with him in their garden after school.

B ▶ Listen and tick (✔) the box.

Example Which is Lily's house?

A ☐   B ☐   C ✔

1 What is Dan's father doing now?

A ☐   B ☐   C ☐

2 What are Lily and Dan playing?

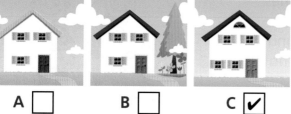

A ☐   B ☐   C ☐

3 How does Dan's mother go to work?

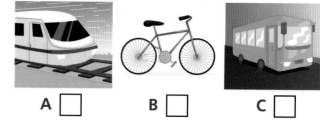

A ☐   B ☐   C ☐

4 What is on Mr Field's balcony?

A ☐   B ☐   C ☐

5 Who is waiting at the bus stop?

A ☐   B ☐   C ☐

C ▶ **Listen to us!**

My son, my brother, my mother and my uncle are waiting in Upunder Road for the number one bus.

D **Read and choose the best answer.**

Example

Dan: What's the new girl's name?
Lily: (A) It's Sally Love.
B No, Pat's 10 now.
C Lily can't come.

Questions

1 Dan: What's she like?
Lily: A She likes chocolate.
B It's her new tablet.
C She's really nice.

2 Dan: Has she got any brothers?
Lily: A Only one, I think.
B She never does that.
C No, it's Charlie.

3 Dan: Tell me about her.
Lily: A Some really loud music!
B She's good at sport!
C It's my paper, not hers!

4 Dan: What's she good at in class?
Lily: A Yes, she thinks it's great.
B She can spell long words.
C It's better than this lesson.

5 Dan: Shall I invite her to my party?
Lily: A So do I!
B Good idea!
C Here you are!

6 Dan: What's her phone number?
Lily: A Yes, she's in class 13.
B Her phone's really great.
C I don't know, but I can ask her.

PROJECT

E **Read and draw pictures of Dan, Lily and Sally.**

Dan and Lily both live in Easy Street and now Sally lives there, too. Dan's got brown eyes, but Lily's and Sally's eyes are blue and bigger than Dan's. Dan's got the biggest nose and the biggest ears, but his mouth is the smallest. Dan's hair is brown and really curly, but Lily's is blonde and straight. Sally's hair is black. It's shorter than Lily's hair but it's longer than Dan's hair!

11 Things we eat and drink

A Write the food and drink words in the correct box.

coconut lime burger coffee beans sauce pasta chicken lemonade
carrot mango pancake apple sausage tea egg milk cheese pear
juice chocolate ice cream fish water peas onion lemon rice
milkshake watermelon noodles banana pie meatballs kiwi

chicken
.... **meat**
....
....

...... juice ......
.... **drinks**
....
....

coconut
....
....
....
....
....
....
....
....

VEGETABLES
...... peas ......
....
....

...... pasta ......
....
....
....
....
....

B Say which one is different and why.

Example Soup is different. Soup is hot. Orange juice, lemonade and ice cream aren't hot. They're cold.

hot/cold   meat/fruit
green/orange   eat/drink

C Choose the correct words and write them on the lines.

a pineapple   soup   a sandwich   coffee   sweets   pancakes   a milkshake

Example	This fruit is yellow inside and you can make juice from it.	*a pineapple*
1	Some people put milk and sugar in this hot drink.	....
2	You make this drink with milk and your favourite kind of fruit	....
3	These are hot, thin and round. You can put lemon juice on them.	....
4	Most children and grown ups love eating these but they are bad for your teeth!	....
5	You make this with bread and you can put meat or salad inside.	....
6	You can eat or drink this from a bowl or from a cup.	....

D Choose the correct words and write them on the lines.

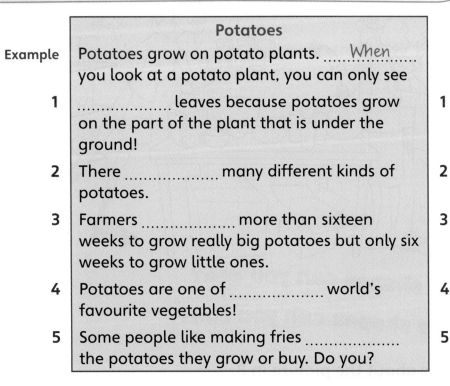

Potatoes

Example Potatoes grow on potato plants. ...*When*... you look at a potato plant, you can only see

1 .... leaves because potatoes grow on the part of the plant that is under the ground!

2 There .... many different kinds of potatoes.

3 Farmers .... more than sixteen weeks to grow really big potatoes but only six weeks to grow little ones.

4 Potatoes are one of .... world's favourite vegetables!

5 Some people like making fries .... the potatoes they grow or buy. Do you?

	What	Which	When
1	its	hers	his
2	is	are	was
3	need	needs	needing
4	a	all	the
5	by	off	with

E Talk in pairs about the food you eat. Then, find words in words!

12 Party things

A What are these? What do we put inside them? Write words.

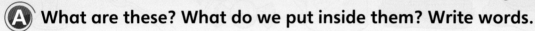

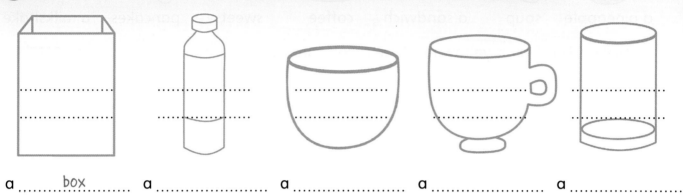

a ......box......   a ....   a ....   a ....   a ....

B ▶ Listen and colour and write.

How many round shapes can you see?

How many square shapes can you see?

C Complete the sentences about the picture in B.

> round   floor   ~~table~~   boxes   bowl   square

1   Three people are standing near a ......table...... in a supermarket.
2   Most of the bottles and .... are on the shelves.
3   The biggest box is on the .... and it is closed.
4   The .... bottle is next to the bigger bowl.
5   Four glasses are between the .... bottle and the smaller ....

D What does Sam have to do? Listen and write words.

Dad's birthday party!
I must

1	phone:	.... Jim this afternoon
2	buy:	.... bottles of lemonade
3	wash:	the three purple ....
4	choose:	some great ....
5	find:	my ....

E Look at the pictures. Tell the story.

Sam

HAPPY BIRTHDAY DAD!

F Read and draw the birthday party table.

Draw a huge table. It can be round or square – you choose!

Draw some glasses, bowls, bottles and plates on top of the table.

On the outside of one of the bottles, write what is inside.

Draw a big birthday cake on a really big square plate.

Draw a birthday present on the floor. You choose the shape!

Add lots of balloons to the picture!

Colour the picture.

13 Different homes

A Draw lines between the words in the boxes and picture A.

door   leaves   trees   wall   roof   chimney

window   basement   balcony   stairs   mat   grass

B Read and choose the best answer.

Example

Sally: Hi Mark! I had lots of fun this afternoon!

Mark: A Tell me about it!
      B How about Saturday?
      C It's better in the morning.

Questions

1 Sally: I went to that big old house where my uncle works.

Mark: A Yes, that's wrong.
      B I know that place.
      C Sorry, I can't.

2 Sally: They're making a movie inside the house!

Mark: A Here they are.
      B How exciting!
      C It's not brave.

3 Sally: There were lots of famous people there today!

Mark: A Really?
      B I'm silly.
      C Shall I?

4 Mark: Is your uncle in the movie?

Sally: A No, you mustn't.
       B It's too scary.
       C Yes, he is!

5 **Sally:** I helped the cameraman today!

    Mark: A No thanks.

            B Well done!

            C Come on!

6 **Sally:** I can show you part of the movie on my phone!

    Mark: A Fantastic!

            B Me too!

            C Be careful!

C **Use 1, 2 or 3 words to complete the sentences about Sally's afternoon.**

Example Sally and Mark are talking about the things that Sally did this
.... *afternoon* ....

1 Sally's uncle works in a ....

2 The people inside the house are making ....

3 Sally saw some .... there.

4 Sally worked with the .... today.

5 Sally and Mark can watch part of the scary movie on Sally's ....

D **Find the differences between the pictures.**

E **Talk about the differences between the pictures.**

1  **2**  **3**  **4**

F **Funtime** **Play the game! Two things.**

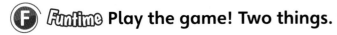

PROJECT

14 Our homes

A **Choose words from the circle to complete what Jack says.**

My .... is Jack Fine.
My .... is 78, Garden
Road. I live in a ....
in a village called Well. Our
home has six ....
We've got a kitchen, a living
room and a dining room
downstairs and two bedrooms
and a bathroom upstairs.

people

address   rooms

tree   name

house

B ▶ **Listen and write.**

Ben's grandmother's new home

Colour: blue and ....._white_.....

1   Number of bedrooms: ....
2   Address: ......, Cook Road
3   Name of village: ....
4   Favourite room: ....
5   House is near: ....

C **Now write about your home.**

I live in .... (an apartment / a flat / a house)
My address is ....
I live in .... (a village / a town / a city / the countryside)
Our home has .... rooms. We've got a ....
....
....
My favourite room is .... because ....
There's a .... near my home. You can .... there.

32

D Answer the questions about where you live.

1 How many windows are there? ....
2 How many phones are there? ....
3 How many floors are there? ....
4 Have you got a garden? ....
5 Does it have a lift? ....
6 Does it have stairs? ....
7 What colour is the roof? ....
8 What's in your living room? ....
....

E Look at the shapes. Spell chicken and kitchen!

t

n

k

i

c

e

h

A ⬠⬜⬠△ is a kind of bird but it can't fly.

We eat in our ⬜⬜☆◯△ because we haven't

got a dining room in our house.

Can you say it?

Charlie the chicken is in Kim's kitchen. Charlie's eating the chips that Kim cooked. Quick! Catch Charlie!

F Listen and draw. Who lives here?

G Draw and describe! My dream home.

PROJECT

15 At our school

(A) Choose the correct words below and write them on the lines.

Example   You can play different kinds of this on a guitar or piano.   ...... *music* ......

1   This is on the classroom wall and the teacher writes on it.   ....
2   These are in books and often have numbers on them at
    the bottom.   ....
3   When you make a mistake with your pencil, you need this.   ....
4   Some teachers put these at the end of correct answers in tests.   ....
5   We look at these to find roads and rivers and towns.   ....

Example

music	a board	maps	a rubber	pages

ticks	pointed	talked	happy

(B) Read the story. Write the correct word from A next to numbers 1–5.

On Tuesday morning, the ...... *music* ...... teacher, Mr Skip, came into Nick's class and said, 'Hello! I've got a message for you from Miss Sweet. She'd like you to answer the questions on (1) .... 66 and 67 for your homework. They're about the world's longest rivers.

Miss Sweet isn't in school today. She's talking on the radio about playing word and picture games in school lessons. It's very exciting!'

Mr Skip (2) .... to some orange books. 'The maps in those can help you, or you can find your answers on the internet,' he said. Nick was (3) .... because he loved working on computers. That evening he found all the answers to Miss Sweet's questions on one of his favourite websites.

When Miss Sweet came back to school, she (4) .... about her exciting day, then looked at everyone's homework. 'What great answers!' she said. 'You've got lots of (5) .... and no crosses! Well done!

Now choose the best name for the story. Tick (✔) one box.

Miss Sweet buys a new radio!   ☐

Nick's class get all the right answers!   ☐

Mr Skip's exciting music lesson!   ☐

C ▶ **Listen and draw lines.**

Alex   Jack   Paul   Daisy

Grace   Hugo   Fred

D **Look and read and write.**

Examples   The clock shows that it's two ....*o'clock*................ .
               What's the boy by the table doing? ....*reading a green book*............ .

Complete the sentences. Write 1, 2, 3, 4 or 5 words.

1   The boy in the blue shirt is ....
2   There are blue and white squares on ....

Answer the questions. Write 1, 2, 3, 4 or 5 words.

3   What's the girl with long black hair looking at?   ....
4   What's the boy with the camera doing?   ....

Now write one sentence about the picture.

5   ....

E **Colour your answers.**

1   How do you come to school?   by (bike car bus train) (I walk)

2   Where do you do your homework?   in the (bedroom library kitchen living room)

3   When do you have English lessons?   on (Monday Tuesday Wednesday Thursday Friday Saturday)

4   What do you like doing most in English?   (speaking writing listening reading)

F **Funtime Play the game! Backs to the board.**

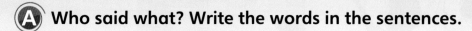

16 Let's do some sport!

A Who said what? Write the words in the sentences.

Vicky

watched   laughed
shouted   watched
played   ~~played~~   jumped
jumped   shouted
rained

FRED

I enjoyed Saturday! I ....._played_..... tennis in the morning and .... a DVD in the afternoon. In the evening, our dog .... in some water. Dad .... 'Don't do that!' But it was funny. I .... a lot!

Sunday was OK. I .... hockey in the morning and I .... a football game on TV in the afternoon. But my mouse .... out of its box in the evening and Mum .... 'Help!' It .... a lot too.

B ▶ Mrs Ship is talking to Alice about her family and their hobbies. Which is each person's favourite hobby? Listen and write a letter in each box.

her mother
☐ C

her son
☐

her sister
☐

her uncle
☐

her daughter
☐

her cousin
☐

A

B

C

D

E

F

G

H

C Find the answers to the questions. Write numbers.

Alice is telling Mrs Ship about a sport which she played.

(1) What game did you play?   ◯ Yes, it was great!

(2) When?   ◯ Baseball!

(3) Was it fun?   ◯ On Friday.

D Choose the correct words and write them on the lines.

	Football				
Example	People all round ....*the*.... world play		the	as	this
1	football but the first people .... played football lived in England. Did you know that in many games, football players	1	whose	what	who
2	.... about eight kilometres!	2	run	runs	running
	The game is called football in most countries but in America and Canada some people				
3	call .... soccer. Another name for football is 'the beautiful game'.	3	them	it	us
	One of the most famous football players is called Lionel Messi. He's a fantastic player.				
4	He could kick a ball really well .... he was only five. You can read about him	4	when	because	or
5	.... the internet.	5	by	at	on

E Write the sport. You can make all the words from the letters in the sport.
(The first letter of the first word is the first letter of the sport!)

Example	b a s k e t b a l l	ball, table, ask
1	_ _ _ _ _ _ _ _	fall, boat, too, boot
2	_ _ _ _ _ _ _ _ _ _ _	tail, net, best, table
3	_ _ _ _ _ _ _ _ _	bad, bat, into, mat
4	_ _ _ _ _ _ _ _ _ _	in, nice, sing, tick, skate
5	_ _ _ _ _ _ _ _ _ _ _	hide, doing, goes, ride

How many words can you make from

sports centre

PROJECT

F Choose your sport!

17 Our hobbies

A Listen and draw lines.

Sally   Peter   Pat   Charlie

Mary   Julia   Matt

B Write the words under the pictures. The first letter is there to help you.

1 ....hockey....   2 ice s................   3 c................   4 D................

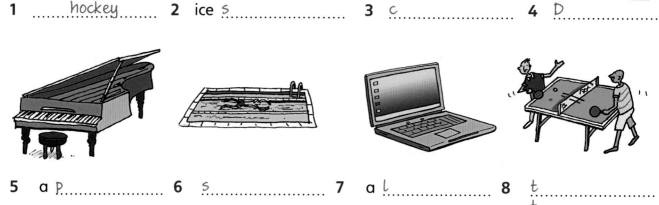

5 a p................   6 s................   7 a l................   8 t................
t................

C Choose the correct words from B and write them on the lines.

1   This is like dancing but you do it on ice.   *skating*
2   You can do this after you jump into a lake or a pool.   ....
3   There are funny stories and lots of pictures in these.   ....
4   You can play music on this. Part of it is black and white.   ....
5   These are films you can watch on a computer.   ....
6   People hit a small ball that bounces in this game.   ....
7   It's easy to carry this kind of computer in your school bag.   ....

D Choose words from B. Write the correct words next to numbers 1–5.

Clare is my younger sister. She loves her new tablet but she likes doing sports like ....*hockey*........... outside more. She practises every Friday after school.

Clare likes sunny weather but last weekend, it snowed and Clare went ice (1) .... on the lake in the park with her friends.

Dan, my older brother, doesn't like hot weather and enjoys being inside. He likes finding new apps and listening to music on his radio or (2) ....

Last Saturday, he watched two new (3) .... at home with his friends. The only sport Dan plays is (4) .... in our basement with his best friend Mark.

When he's older, Dan wants to draw the kind of pictures you sometimes see in (5) .... or on children's websites. He's very good at that.

E Now choose the best name for the story about Clare and Dan. Tick (✔) one box.

My brother and sister ☐   A day at the park ☐   My favourite sport ☐

F ▶ Listen, then tell the three word story!

Julia's beach day

home, cupboard, bags
bags, car, beach
beach, got out, hat
hat, towel, bags
bags, hello, Matt
Matt, boat, sea
Julia, went to sleep, sun

G Funtime Play the game! Draw your circle.

18 At the hospital

A Look and read. Choose the correct words and write them on the lines.

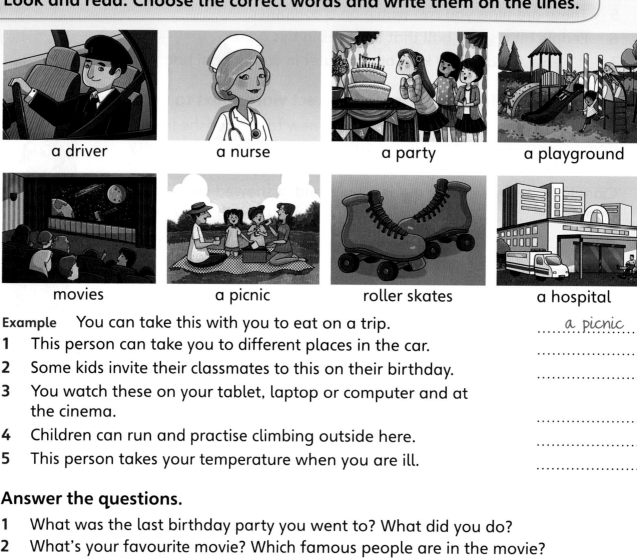

a driver   a nurse   a party   a playground

movies   a picnic   roller skates   a hospital

Example You can take this with you to eat on a trip. .... *a picnic* ....
1 This person can take you to different places in the car. ....
2 Some kids invite their classmates to this on their birthday. ....
3 You watch these on your tablet, laptop or computer and at
   the cinema. ....
4 Children can run and practise climbing outside here. ....
5 This person takes your temperature when you are ill. ....

B Answer the questions.

1 What was the last birthday party you went to? What did you do?
2 What's your favourite movie? Which famous people are in the movie?
3 What food and drink do you take when you have a picnic?
4 What's the name of the nearest hospital? Is it a big hospital?
5 Is someone in your family a dentist, a nurse or a doctor?

C Choose the best words and complete the sentences.

1 Sometimes, when you are not .... and
   your body is ...., you have a temperature.

   > hot   well
   > cold   sick

2 When your mum has a .... headache,
   it's a good idea to be very .... at home.

   > bad   asleep
   > quiet   tired

3 Be .... when you're hungry! Sam ate five
   huge chocolate ice creams on Sunday and then he had a
   .... stomach-ache!

   > dirty   terrible
   > brave   careful

D Look and read and write.

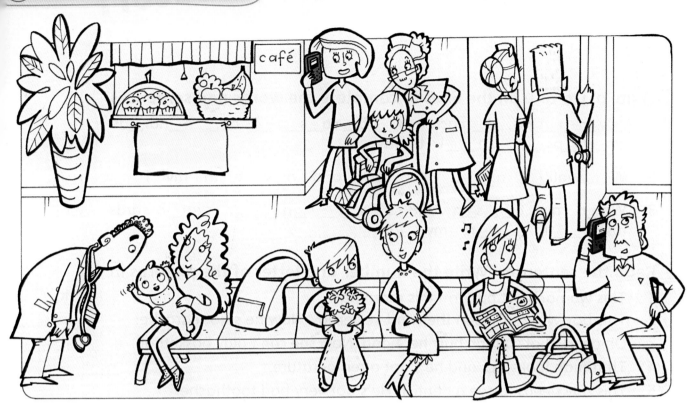

Examples These people are in a ....hospital.............. .
     What is the boy on the seat holding? ..some beautiful flowers.. .

Complete the sentences. Write 1, 2, 3, 4 or 5 words.

1 In the café, you can buy ....
2 One of the girls is reading ....

Answer the questions. Write 1, 2, 3, 4 or 5 words.

3 What is the man with the red phone doing? ....
4 Who is smiling at the baby? ....

Now write two sentences about the picture.

5 ....
6 ....

E Listen and colour and write.

F Funtime Play the game! Find the silent letters.

temp**e**rature sick

stomach   talk

building friends head

19 What is the matter?

A Write e, i, o or u on the lines to complete the words and sentences.

1 __'v__ g__t a st__mach-ach__ b__ ca__s__ __ at__ h__ndr__ds
of ch__ps at sch__ __l t__day.

2 W__ walk__d a l__t y__st__rday and n__w b__th my f__ __t h__rt.

3 Wh__n my c__ __s__n and I w__r__ __n __ __r skat__b__ards
last w__ __k, I h__rt my ....

B Read the sentences. Write the number and letter of the pictures in C.

1	This woman hurt her arm this morning.	........4C...........
2	This boy was outside in the wind yesterday. Now he's got earache.	....
3	Oh dear! That woman hurt her hand. Now she can't play basketball.	....
4	That man looks sick and he's got a temperature.	....
5	This boy needs to see a dentist. He's got very bad toothache.	....
6	That farmer tried to fix his tractor. Now his back hurts.	....
7	Give that girl a glass of water, please! She's got a cough.	....
8	That man had four milkshakes. Now he's got a stomach-ache.	....

C ▶ Listen and tick (✔) the box.

1 What is the matter with Ben?

A ☐   B ☐   C ☐

2 What was the matter with Kim today?

A ☐   B ☐   C ☐

3 What is the matter with Dad?

A ☐   B ☐   C ☐

4 Why did Mum go to hospital?

A ☐   B ☐   C ☐

D Read and choose the best answer.

Example

Zoe: Hello, Tom. How are you?

Tom: (A) I'm OK!

     B Well done!

     C That's cool!

Questions

1 Zoe: Why weren't you at school today?

  Tom: A That is today's lesson.

       B It's in our building.

       C I went to hospital.

2 Zoe: What was the matter?

  Tom: A It's not mine.

       B I hurt my foot.

       C You asked me.

3 Tom: The nurse was really nice.

  Zoe: A Was she?

       B Here you are!

       C Where is it?

4 Zoe: So, are you all right?

  Tom: A Yes! Don't worry!

       B I can walk there!

       C OK, I can tell you!

5 Zoe: What are you doing now?

  Tom: A I'd like to do that a lot.

       B I'm watching TV.

       C It's next to the phone.

6 Zoe: Can I come and see you?

  Tom: A Yes, I often do that.

       B Yes, that's a great idea.

       C Yes, she came yesterday.

E Find five differences between Tom and Paul.

Tom

F Answer the questions about Paul. Write 1, 2, 3, 4 or 5 words.

1 Why didn't Paul come to school today?   *He went to hospital.*

2 What is the matter with him?

3 How did he do that?

4 What is Paul dreaming about?

5 What is his book about?

6 What does he want to do when he's OK again?

G Saying 'ch'.

Charlie chose a cheese sandwich for lunch.
Kim ate a lot of carrot cake then she had a stomach-ache!

20 Where?

(A) **Write the words under the pictures.**

> a shop   a lift   a farm   a supermarket   a car park   the sea   a river   a market
> stairs   a hospital   a cinema   a beach   a mountain   a playground   a lake   a funfair

1

a   *a playground*   b   c   ....   d   ....

2

a   ....   b   c   ....   d   ....

3

a   ....   b   c   ....   d   ....

4

a   ....   b   c   ....   d   ....

5

   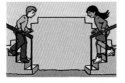      

a   ....   b   c   ....   d   ....

(B) **Which picture is different and why?**

C **Read the story. Choose a word from the box. Write the correct word next to numbers 1–5.**

Example

sunny   sandwiches   give   afraid

work   walk   loud   lake   doctor

Fred and Grace live in the town centre but on ....*sunny*........ days, they sometimes go for bike rides in the countryside. Last Saturday, they rode to a little
(1) .... and jumped about on the rocks next to the water there. Fred saw three ducks on a small island. 'Come here, ducks!' he shouted. But the ducks didn't come because they were (2) .... of the noise. 'Don't worry about the ducks now, Fred!' Grace said. 'Let's sit down on our rug. I've got some apple juice in my bag to drink. Do you want some?', she asked. 'Yes! I'm really thirsty,' Fred answered. 'Let's eat all our cheese (3) .... now, too.

Grace took the food out of her bag. 'Look!' she said. Those ducks aren't frightened now. They can see our picnic! Let's feed them. We can (4) .... them some of our bread.'

'Good idea!' said Fred. 'Come on, you silly ducks! There's lots for you to eat here!

'I love animals!' Grace laughed. 'I want to be a (5) .... one day – but I'd like to help sick animals get better more than people, I think.'

Choose the best name for the story. Tick (✔) one box.

Grace's new bike   ☐

Mum has a picnic   ☐

Fred's duck friends   ☐

D **Make your pictures the same!**

E **Find the 'k's! Look at the words in A and C. Put a line under all the 'k's you find.**

21 Here and there in town

A Where can you go to do these things in town?

go for a swim   **catch buses**   **buy a milkshake**
laugh at clowns   **choose books**   **see a doctor**

B Look and read. Choose the correct words and write them on the lines.

a supermarket   coffee   soup   a café

a zoo   milk   a hospital   grapes

Example	People go here to see different animals like tigers, zebras and penguins.	a zoo
1	You can make this from vegetables then put it in a bowl.	....
2	People sit and have a drink and talk to their friends here.	....
3	This fruit can be red or green. You can eat it or drink its juice.	....
4	You can buy lots of different food in this large store.	....
5	Mothers often give this white drink to babies.	....

C Read Eva's postcard and write the correct words.

Hi Grandpa!

It's great here!

We didn't go to the beach this morning. We drove to the town to go for a walk there. We had lunch there too. We found a café near the market with lots of chairs outside. Mum had pea soup and Dad and I had meatballs and salad. Then we went to the market to buy some kiwis. Mum bought a new swimsuit there too.

It's the end of the afternoon now and we're in the park. Mum's asleep under a big tree! Dad isn't. He's waiting to play badminton now! I've got to go! See you!

Love Eva XX

meatballs
walked ~~town~~
tennis pea soup
badminton asleep
shopping market

1 Eva and her family went to the ....*town*........ this morning.
2 Eva's mother had .... in a café that was near the market.
3 Eva had .... with some salad in the café.
4 The family bought some fruit and a swimsuit at the ....
5 Eva's mother is .... in the park now.
6 Eva's father wants to have a game of .... in the park.

D ▶ Listen and tick (✔) the box.

Example Where does May's brother work?

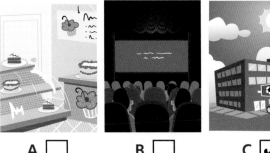

A ☐   B ☐   C ✔

1 Which is Kim's dad?

A ☐   B ☐   C ☐

2 Where did Dan have lunch?

A ☐   B ☐   C ☐

3 What is Lily doing?

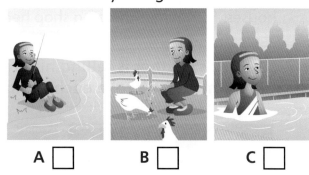

A ☐   B ☐   C ☐

4 What is Aunt Lucy doing?

A ☐   B ☐   C ☐

5 Where is Charlie's bag?

A ☐   B ☐   C ☐

E Listen and say!

Super soup, juice and beautiful fruit too for you at the new Super Food Supermarket!

F *Funtime* Play the game! Connecting words.

22 A trip to the city

A Write sentences about a village and a city.

A village

Not many people live here

A city

Thousands of people live here. Homes are often newer. Most buildings are taller. People often walk more quickly. Streets are often longer here. It's quieter here. Sometimes farms are near here. Roads are often shorter. There are big shopping centres. People often walk more slowly. Homes are often older. It's noisier here. Not many people have tall houses. Sometimes there's a shop here. Schools have lots of classrooms.

B ▶ Jack's mother is telling him to take things to different parts of the city. Where must Jack take each thing? Listen and write a letter in each box.

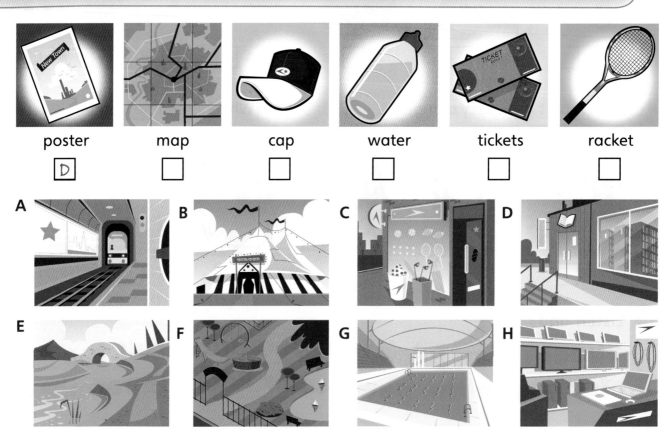

poster	map	cap	water	tickets	racket
D	☐	☐	☐	☐	☐

A   B   C   D

E   F   G   H

48

C **I think I know the answer!**
Is the right answer green or purple?

So do I.

I think this city is a really exciting place!

Because he's funny.

Do you want to go there?

I know there is a bookshop near here.

Yes, in my aunt's bookcase.

No, it isn't in this road.

I think we need to find a café. I'm hungry!

And I'm really thirsty!

Outside the shopping centre.

I know that's the right bus. Quick! Come on!

OK! Let's run!

D **Look and read and write.**

Examples   You can see a bus stop between two .... *shops* ....
                  What is the girl in the yellow helmet doing?   *riding a purple bike* .

Complete the sentences. Write 1, 2, 3, 4 or 5 words.

1   Two children are carrying ....
2   The girl with long blonde hair is ....

Answer the questions. Write 1, 2, 3 4 or 5 words.

3   What is in the tree?   ....
4   What is the clown wearing?   ....

Now write two sentences about the picture.

5   ....
6   ....

23 The world around us

A Draw circles round the things that you can see in the picture.

a farm	fields	flowers	rocks	a car park
grass	an island	a jungle	stars	mountains
clouds	the moon	a waterfall	plants	a path

B Look at the picture and read. What are these sentences about?

1 People like walking or climbing up these when they are on holiday. ....
2 You can swim and sail here, but it is not a river or the sea. ....
3 There are always lots of trees, animals and birds here. ....
4 You find these on trees and plants. They are green, red, yellow or brown. ....
5 People live in their homes here but it's smaller than a town. ....
6 Go outside in the day, look up and see this! It's big, hot, yellow and round. ....

C ▶ Listen and colour and write.

D **Read and cross out the wrong words.**

Jungles

Jungles are (1) *cold / hot*, and (2) *dry / wet* places. They are very (3) *green / pink / black* because it (4) *never / often / carefully* rains there. A lot of fantastic flowers, plants and (5) *animals / puppies / pets* live in jungles. There are big (6) *rivers / seas / streets* in lots of jungles. Be careful, because sometimes you can find dangerous (7) *crocodiles / whales / dolphins* in some of them!

Many people who live in a jungle have their homes next to a river or a waterfall because they need to drink its (8) *soup / tea / water*. People often travel up or down the river by (9) *boat / truck / motorbike*. Rivers are like roads in a jungle.

E **Write g or j to complete the words, then say the sentences!**

There are some _g_reat __reen __rapes in __race's __randma's __arden.

_J_ill's hu__e __iraffe en__oys ve__etables and __ungle __uice!

F 𝕱𝖚𝖓𝖙𝖎𝖒𝖊 **Do the *World Around Us* quiz!**

24 Travelling, texting, phoning

A **Look at picture a. What do you think? Write yes or no.**

1   The man is in the countryside. ....
2   It's a very cloudy day. ....
3   Two things are flying in this picture. ....
4   The man came to this place by car. ....
5   The weather is really cold there. ....

a

B **Picture a or b? Read the sentences and write a or b.**

1   There are no leaves on the trees. ....b....
2   There's only one cloud. ....
3   The helicopter is on the ground. ....
4   The man's hair is straight. ....
5   You can see a red car. ....
6   The duck is bigger. ....
7   The man is pointing at the helicopter. ....
8   The red and white rug is square. ....
9   The man is wearing a blue shirt. ....

b

C **Complete the sentences.**

1   In picture **a**, there's one cloud, but in picture **b**, there are ....two........ clouds.
2   In picture **b**, the man's got blond hair, but in **a**, he's got .... hair.
3   In **b**, the picnic rug is square, but in **a**, it's ....
4   In picture **a**, the helicopter's flying, but in **b**, it's on the ....
5   In picture **b**, the car's .... , but in picture **a**, it's ....
6   In **a**, the man's shirt is .... , but in **b**, it's ....
7   In picture **a**, the trees have got .... , but in **b**, they ....

D Write the letters of the alphabet to complete the words.

a																									z
				5					10															25	

1   13 5 19 19 1 7 5
    m e s s a g e

2   9 14 20 5 18 14 5 20
    i n t _ r n _ _

3   5 13 1 9 12
    _ _ _ _ _ l

4   20 5 24 20
    _ _ x _

5   1 16 16
    _ _ _

6   23 5 2 19 9 20 5
    w _ b _ _ _ _ _

7   16 8 15 20 15 19
    p h _ _ _ _ _

8   20 1 2 12 5 20
    _ _ _ _ _ _

9   5 2 15 15 11
    _ - _ _ _ _

E Write the words from D in Nick's sentences.

Nick is phoning his work friend May to tell her about his trip.

I'm calling you because I sent you a (4) ....text........ this morning but I don't think you got my (1) ....

No, I didn't.

And I can't (3) .... you because there's no (2) .... here.

Don't worry!

I've got lots of (7) .... and videos on my (8) .... because I'm taking pictures of everything and filming things too.

Great!

I'd like to add the (7) .... and videos to our (6) ....

Good idea!

Oh! And I found a really exciting (5) .... It's really cool! I'd like to show it to you.

OK! Brilliant!

F Let's find things that we all like and do!

25 Which one is different?

A Write words for the pictures, draw another picture and complete the sentence.

1 A ......plane......,
   a .... and
   a .... can fly.

2 All these men have got
   ....

3 The ....,
   the .... and the
   .... are yellow.

4 You can find an ....,
   a .... and a
   .... in a living room.

B Say which picture is different and why.

1

2

3

4

5

54

C Read the story. Choose a word from the box. Write the correct word next to numbers 1–5.

Daisy ....*loved*........ animals. Lots of her friends had pets and Daisy wanted one too. One day she read a story in a (1) .... about a boy who had a donkey. Daisy had an idea. 'Mum,' she said, 'Donkeys are so funny! Can we (2) .... a donkey?'

'Sorry, Daisy,' her mother answered. 'We can't have a donkey. We haven't got a field.' 'What about a kitten or a penguin, then?' Daisy asked. 'My friend, Sally, has got a cat.' 'No!' her mother said. 'Don't be silly, Daisy. We (3) .... in a flat. Cats like being in gardens and penguins like being near water. Sorry!'

Daisy went and sat on the balcony. She wasn't happy. She sat down on the ground next to a snail. 'Snails aren't very good pets,' she thought. But then she saw a really sweet grey lizard between the two pretty green (4) .... there. 'Hello!' she said. 'Do you want to be my new pet?' The lizard looked at Daisy and moved its (5) .... up and down. 'Wow! It's saying yes!' laughed Daisy. 'It's different from all my friends' pets, but that's OK!'

Example

loved   head   plants   grey   cloudy

buy   downstairs   comic   live

Now choose the best name for the story. Tick (✔) one box.

Sally moves to a different flat ☐   Daisy finds a pet ☐   Mum writes a story ☐

D Choose words for the donkey and the cat.

Daisy's lizard was *really sweet* and the plants were *pretty and green*.

Now choose words for the boy's donkey and Sally's cat:

Daisy read a story about a boy who had	a	nice	big	black	donkey.
			little	brown	
		beautiful	strong	grey	
Daisy's friend Sally has got	an	ugly	clever	orange	cat.
			naughty	white	

E Funtime Play the game! Make groups of words.

26 Guess who lives here?

A Look and read and write.

(..............) (..............) (..............) (..............) (..............)

Examples The window at the back of the room is .... *closed* ....
What is tall and brown and opposite the stairs? .... *the old clock* ....

Complete the sentences. Write 1, 2, 3, 4 or 5 words.

1 On the wall, there is a picture of a ....
2 The bat on the desk is next to ....

Answer the questions. Write 1, 2, 3, 4 or 5 words.

3 What is the bat at the bottom of the stairs doing? ....
4 Which animal has got eight legs? ....

Now write two sentences about the picture.

5 ....
6 ....

B Listen and write the names of the bats.
Then, draw lines between the names and the bats.

C Read and then write the names of the people who live in each flat.

Mr and Mrs White live at the bottom of the stairs, below Mary Pink. Mr White is a cook and likes cooking a lot at home too. They often invite friends to their flat and they have dinner parties.

Anna and Bill Brown love reading quietly in their living room. They don't like living above Miss Green because she plays very loud music when she comes home after work.

Miss Green lives opposite her friend Mary Pink. They are both learning to play the guitar and they make a lot of noise.

Mark Grey's flat is under Miss Green's. He doesn't have to drive to work because he works on his website at home but he puts on his roller skates and skates around the park every morning first.

The newest person in this house is Julia Blue. She moved into the flat at the top of the stairs, two floors above Mr and Mrs White's apartment. She loves skateboarding and wants to be a pop star.

D Funtime Play the game! Alphabet find and draw.

E From top to bottom!

PROJECT

57

27 Seeing differences

A **Make sentences about the things in the pictures.**

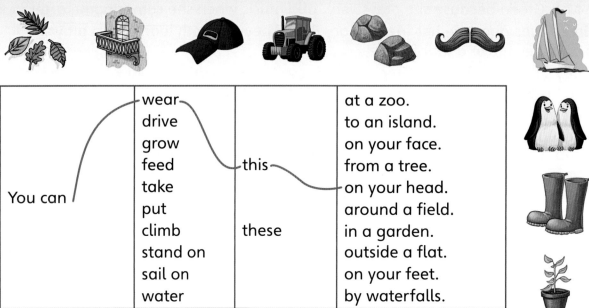

| You can | wear
drive
grow
feed
take
put
climb
stand on
sail on
water | this

these | at a zoo.
to an island.
on your face.
from a tree.
on your head.
around a field.
in a garden.
outside a flat.
on your feet.
by waterfalls. |

B **Find the words in the box and write them on the lines.**

Example   This is green and cows and horses eat it.   ....grass.......

1   You see this on the ground at the beach.   ....

2   People sometimes wear these when the weather is hot,
      or for football practice.   ....

3   Bands sometimes write these. They're music with words.   ....

4   Some people have these when they are asleep.   ....

5   You can call people on this and
      talk to them.   a ....

6   This can grow under a man's
      nose and above his mouth.   a ....

7   You run a lot and kick a ball in
      this game.   ....

8   This is hair that grows below
      men's mouths.   a ....

d	r	e	a	m	s	m
n	b	e	a	r	d	o
s	h	o	r	t	s	u
g	l	a	s	s	e	s
s	o	c	c	e	r	t
b	v	s	a	n	d	a
i	s	o	n	g	s	c
k	p	h	o	n	e	h
e	g	r	a	s	s	e

C Say which picture is different and why.

D Listen and write your answers, then complete the story.

Hi! This morning, I watched a video on my laptop of (1) .... who sang
(7) .... very loudly. At eleven o'clock, I ate (5) .... plates of
(4) .... (6) .... because I was really hungry. I didn't go to
(2) .... to play (3) .... with my classmates this afternoon, because
my (9) .... hurt! I went to bed and had a dream about (8) .... silly
(10) .... In my dream, they skipped and hopped outside my room on our
balcony. They danced to (7) .... too! When I woke up, I was OK again! Bye!

E Funtime Play the game! Plural quiz.

28 Our busy holidays

A ▶ **Listen and draw lines and then complete the sentences.**

(Monday) (Tuesday) (Wednesday) (Thursday) (Friday) (Saturday) (Sunday)

1 On ...., Alex climbs mountains and the weather is sometimes
   ....

2 Alex always paints walls with his .... Matt on ....

3 Alex sometimes videos his .... Lucy when she plays basketball on
   ....

4 Alex always has helicopter lessons with his .... Eva on
   ....

5 Fridays are exciting too because Alex and his uncle ....

B **Answer the questions.**

1 Where do you go in
   the school holidays?

A ☐   B ☐   C ☐

2 What do you wear?

A ☐   B ☐   C ☐

3 Who do you see?   my family   my friends   my teacher

A ☐   B ☐   C ☐

C **Choose a word from the box. Write the correct word next to numbers 1–5.**

Hi! Alex is my dad. I'm called .... and I'm ten. My brother ....
is a year younger than I am.

In the school holidays, our parents always take us to exciting places like funfairs
and circuses but I enjoy going to the beach best! We often go ..... *sailing* ..... on
our boat there. We love (1) .... and playing in the water. We like fishing
in the (2) .... too, but we never catch any big fish!

Our dog, Jack, always comes with us. Sometimes, we (3) .... Jack's ball
and he tries to find it. He loves doing that! Last year we took Jack on a balloon
and helicopter ride! When he was a puppy, Jack was really (4) .... of
flying, but now he isn't!

We like watching movies on Dad's laptop or Mum's tablet and playing video
(5) .... on the internet. We've got lots of apps on our phones too. One
teaches me new words. But we don't do those things in the school holidays
because we think it's more exciting to be outside.

What do you like doing in your school holidays?

Example			
sailing	song	hide	swimming
frightened	tennis	games	river	pretty

D **Write the correct words on the lines then ask four questions.**

...... *make* ...... a cake   ...... *eat* ...... a cake
drink a ....   go .... for clothes
read an ....   listen to your favourite ....
phone your best ....   go for a long ....
drive a .... by plane

~~make~~ ~~eat~~ shopping tractor travel
friend walk band milkshake e-book

E 🄵🄷🄽🄻🄸🄼🄴 **Play the game! Who, what, when, where?**

29 About us

A Look at the pictures. Complete the sentences.

That man sings very
....

That man is
driving very
....

B What do you think? Write yes or no.

1   People in my country drive slowly.   ....
2   Everyone in my family talks quietly.   ....
3   I always carry things carefully.   ....
4   My parents dance very badly.   ....
5   Our teacher sings really well.   ....
6   Our class is learning English very quickly. ....
7   Music is better when people play it loudly. ....

yes answers [   ]   no answers [   ]

C Find words that start with these letters in the picnic picture.

c d p

D ▶ Listen and draw lines.

Mary   Dan   Daisy   Sally

Fred   Bill   Vicky

E Read the story. Choose words.

Dan's trip to the castle

I walked to the castle quickly / (slowly). My feet hurt because I (1) had / didn't have any boots or shoes on!

When I got to the castle, I bought a big lemon ice cream because I (2) was / wasn't hot and hungry. But then, because I (3) held / didn't hold it carefully, I dropped it! I was angry after that. I (4) sat / didn't sit down on a seat inside the castle because I was really tired after my long walk. I went to sleep and had a dream.

In my dream, a monster came into the castle, looked at me and then shouted something very (5) loudly / quietly. I was (6) dangerous / surprised but I wasn't (7) frightened / thirsty because the monster smiled at me! He took me into the castle kitchen and gave me some more lemon ice cream in a (8) huge / brave pink bowl. I (9) dropped / didn't drop my ice cream on the floor again because I sat on a seat and (10) ate / didn't eat it slowly. It was the best ice cream in the world!!

F Ask and answer questions.

	Me	....
1 Can you swim under the water?	....	....
2 Are you good at running?	....	....
3 Can you cook rice or noodles?	....	....
4 Do you eat quickly or slowly?	....	....
5 Can you clap really loudly?	....	....
6 Are you good at counting in English?	....	....

G Funtime Play the game! Draw the sentences.

30 About me

A ▶ **Listen and tick (✔) the questions that Miss White asks. Then listen again and write Bill's answers.**

B **Answer questions 1–4. Ask your friend questions 5–12.**

	Bill	you
Let's talk about you.		
1 How old are you?		
2 How many brothers and sisters have you got?		
3 What's your favourite colour?		
4 How often do you see your friends?		
Let's talk about your school.		**your friend**
5 Who do you sit next to in class?		
6 How many lessons do you have?		
7 How do you come to school?		
8 Where do you do your homework?		
9 Which is your favourite school day?		
Let's talk about the things you like.		**your friend**
10 What's your favourite film?		
a *When did you see the film?*		
b *Where did you see it?*		
c *Who did you see the film with?*		
d *Why do you like the film? Is it funny, exciting?*		
11 Do you like music?		
a *Can you play the piano or the guitar?*		
b *Are you good at singing?*		
12 Can you swim?		

C **What is this about? Write the same word in all the boxes!**

[_____] Lessons
— make you cleverer —

In every country in the world, people make and listen to [_____].

In many schools, children have [_____] lessons. In their classes,
they can learn to sing songs and to play [_____] on the piano or guitar.

But did you know that learning [_____] can help your reading,
spelling and maths too?

In the USA, grown-ups tested 90 school children.

Children who had more [_____] and Art lessons got better marks
in Maths. Their reading was better too!

D **Look, read and do!**

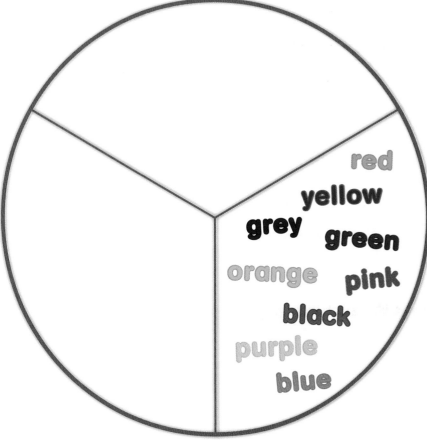

red
yellow
grey green
orange pink
black
purple
blue

1
How many words for colours
are there? Say the colour –
not the word you read!

2
Write the sports that your
class likes playing and
watching in the top part.

3
In the bottom part, write two
of your favourite foods and
put a star * next to them.
Then, write which fruit juice
you like drinking. Draw a
smiley ☺ after that! And last,
write something you <u>don't</u> like
eating. Then, draw a sad face
☹ after that!

E **Funtime** **Play the game! On my right and on my left.**

65

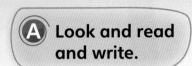

31 Why is Sally crying?

A **Look and read and write.**

Clare

Jim

Sue

Ben

Mary

Fred

Examples Behind the three giraffes, you can see a .... *zebra* .

Why is the girl afraid? .... *She can see a spider* .

Complete the sentences. Write 1, 2, 3, 4 or 5 words.

1   Two boys are pointing and ....

2   The boy on the seat hurt ....

Answer the questions. Write 1, 2, 3, 4 or 5 words.

3   What is the old man wearing? ....

4   What is the robot doing? ....

Now write two sentences about the picture.

5   ....

6   ....

B ▶ **Listen and colour and write.**

C **Listen and draw lines.**

D **Look at the pictures and complete and tell the story.**

1  ....

2  ....

3  ....

4  ...a...

Bill's got a baby sister called Sally. Sally's only four years old. (1) Sally is really
........sad........ because she wants to play with her favourite teddy bear. But her teddy
bear's really .... (2) Sally's teddy bear is in some .... now because
Sally's mum is .... it. (3) Sally's mother is putting the teddy bear outside in the
.... She's putting two wet .... outside too.
(4) Now, Sally is very .... because her teddy bear is dry and very ....

> sad   water   garden   washing   dirty   socks   happy   clean   crying

Write the letters under the correct picture.

Mum says ...
a   Don't worry! Here's your bear, Sally. It's clean again now!
b   Oh dear! I think your bear needs a bath.
c   Your bear's outside in the garden! It's drying in the wind.
d   Your bear was really dirty! Look at this water! It's black!

E **Read about Mr and Mrs Cook's naughty daughter Lily and draw lines.**

What did Lily do this morning?	I know!
Who did she go to the beach with?	Because she got very cold.
When did she come home?	She's having a hot shower.
Where is she now?	Her two new classmates.
Why is she having a hot shower?	She went to the beach.
How did she get cold?	She came home for lunch.
She's a naughty daughter sometimes!	She jumped off a rock into the cold water with all her clothes on.

F **Funtime** **Play the game! Match the cards.**

32 Mary goes shopping

A What's in the kitchen? Make sentences.

There's ...
There are ...

only   a lot of   not much   some   any

B Put a tick (✔) or a (✗) next to the things Mary needs to buy.

potatoes ✔   coffee   tea   rice   pasta   oranges   apples
carrots   cheese   onions   tomatoes   noodles   kiwis

C Complete the sentences about the story.

Picture 1 Mary's at the ......*market*...... . She's buying some fruit and .... for her mum. A man's giving Mary a bag of .... Hugo Pie is next to Mary. He's got his bike with him.

Picture 2 Mary's walking home from the market. But all the .... and .... aren't in her bag! Some of them are on the ground. .... 's going home too. He's behind Mary.

Now, write words from the box on the lines for picture 3.

> angry   market   asleep   surprised   along   everything   home   nothing

Mary's at .... now. Her mum's .... with her because there's .... in her shopping bag. Mary's very sorry. She's .... too! 'I don't understand, Mum! I put .... into the bag at the ....' she says.

Answer the questions about picture 4.

1   Where are Mary and her mum now?   ....
2   Who's outside their house?   ....
3   What's inside the box?   ....
4   Are Mary and her mum happy now?   ....

D Who says this? Write Mary, Mary's mum or Hugo Pie.

1   ....Mary......... : Can I have two kilos of potatoes, please?
2   .... : Where are the fruit and vegetables? This bag is empty!
3   .... : You dropped these fruit and vegetables in the street, I think.
4   .... : Thank you! Now I don't have to go shopping again!

E Choose the correct words and write them on the lines.

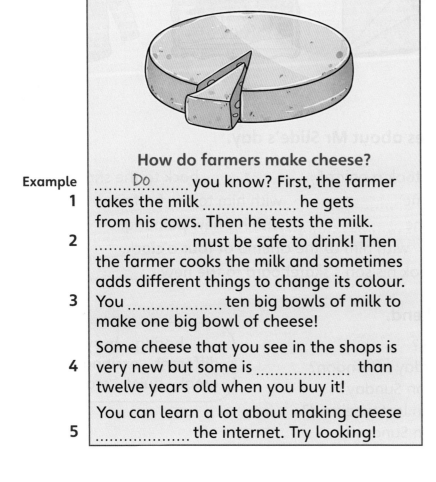

How do farmers make cheese?

		Have	Do	Are
Example	.......Do....... you know? First, the farmer			
1	takes the milk .... he gets from his cows. Then he tests the milk.	**1** what	who	which
2	.... must be safe to drink! Then the farmer cooks the milk and sometimes adds different things to change its colour.	**2** It	We	They
3	You .... ten big bowls of milk to make one big bowl of cheese!	**3** needs	need	needing
4	Some cheese that you see in the shops is very new but some is .... than twelve years old when you buy it!	**4** more	many	most
5	You can learn a lot about making cheese .... the internet. Try looking!	**5** at	on	to

PROJECT

33 Last weekend, last week

A ▶ **Listen and look at the pictures. What did Mr Slide take to each place?**

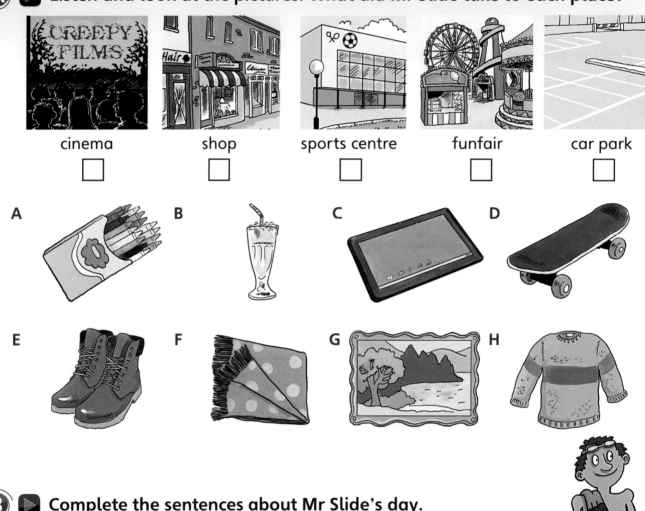

cinema	shop	sports centre	funfair	car park
☐	☐	☐	☐	☐

A   B   C   D

E   F   G   H

B ▶ **Complete the sentences about Mr Slide's day.**

1   In the morning, Mr Slide took a pair of .... back to the shoe shop.
2   Before lunch, he took some .... with him to the funfair.
3   After lunch, he went to the .... with his new painting.
4   He took a .... with him to the cinema at four o'clock.
5   That evening, Mr Slide took his son's skateboard to the new ....

C **Let's talk about last weekend.**

Where were you on Saturday?
Who were you with on Saturday afternoon?
What time did you wake up on Sunday?
What did you do that was fun last weekend?
What was the weather like on Sunday?
Tell me more about last weekend.

> boring   busy   cool
> different   exciting   fantastic
> great   quiet   scary   terrible

Last weekend was .... !

D Read and choose the best answer.

Example

Nick: Did you enjoy your trip last week, Paul?

Paul: (A) It was great!
B Saturday and Sunday!
C What a nice smile!

Questions

1 **Nick:** Which was the best day?
Paul: A Hers is the best one.
B I can go this evening.
C They were all good.

2 **Nick:** How did you travel?
Paul: A There were nine people.
B We went by plane.
C It was very quick.

3 **Nick:** Were you afraid?
Paul: A No, I wasn't.
B It's not mine.
C There isn't any.

4 **Nick:** Was the weather good?
Paul: A Yes! Every day!
B Wow! Hooray!
C Good! Well done!

5 **Nick:** Did you take any photos?
Paul: A I'm OK, thanks.
B No, she doesn't.
C Yes, forty-five!

6 **Nick:** You must show me them!
Paul: A Good night!
B All right!
C I'm sorry.

E Look and find words with *w*!

r	a	i	n	b	o	w	l	s	w	s
s	w	w	h	a	l	e	i	a	i	w
w	e	e	y	c	l	o	w	n	n	i
e	b	e	e	w	o	r	l	d	d	m
a	s	k	l	b	h	t	o	w	n	s
t	i	e	l	r	k	i	w	i	w	u
e	t	n	o	o	c	o	w	c	a	i
r	e	d	w	w	a	t	c	h	v	t
w	a	l	k	n	s	n	o	w	e	e

....
....
....

34 What did you do then?

A Read and circle Fred and Daisy's verbs. Then, add –ed or –d.

jump
call
wait
show
shout
plant
move
play
help
change

When I was young, I walked 50 kilometres in one day, Daisy. Now I only walk to the shops!

When I was a young woman, I climbed mountains, Fred. Now I only climb the stairs to my flat!

B Look at the pictures, then complete the sentences.

1 I p.layed tennis last Monday.
2 My brother p_____ all his friends last night to talk about football.
3 My younger sister c_____ six pictures with her new crayons today.
4 My big sister d_____ to some great music at a party yesterday.
5 My father w_____ a lot at his desk on Tuesday and Wednesday.
6 My cousin Jack s_____ down the river on Saturday.
7 My cousin Alex l_____ a lot at the clowns in the circus yesterday.
8 My uncle Tom c_____ lunch for all the family last Sunday.
9 My older brother d_____ six eggs on the floor last night.
10 My parents c_____ three mountains on their last holiday.

C Look and read and write.

Examples These people are at a ....circus.......... .
What's on the ground between the clown's feet?   ...a green tennis ball...

Complete the sentences. Write 1, 2, 3, 4 or 5 words.

1 The parrot is standing on ....
2 The penguin is ....

Answer the questions. Write 1, 2, 3, 4 or 5 words.

3 Where's the pirate?   ....
4 What's the boy doing?   ....

Now write two sentences about the picture.

5 ....
6 ....

D Complete Jim's message.

day   dressed   shoes   nose   clown

Here we are on Thursday. It was a great ......day......!
My uncle gave me and my friend, Ben, a present.
We opened it and found some .... clothes
inside. We .... up in the clothes. My uncle
put on a big red .... He was really funny!
I put on some really big green .... We all
laughed and laughed!

73

35 What a morning!

A Choose the correct words and write them on the lines.

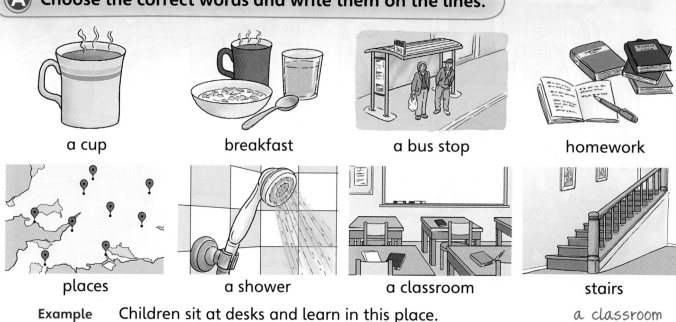

a cup   breakfast   a bus stop   homework

places   a shower   a classroom   stairs

Example   Children sit at desks and learn in this place.   *a classroom*

Questions

1   You can walk up or down these inside your home.   ....

2   Wait here and then a driver takes you to town.   ....

3   You stand in this and wash your body.   ....

4   You put hot coffee in this, then you pick it up and drink from it.   ....

5   You can buy a map or look on the internet to find these.   ....

B Ben's terrible school morning. Look at the pictures. Tell the story.

Ben

C **Read about things we do every day.**
Complete the sentences about Ben's morning.

Every day

We wake up.

Ben's terrible morning

Ben ...._woke_......... up late.

1   We get up and
     we have a shower.

Ben .... up but he
.... a shower.

2   We put on our school clothes and
     have breakfast.

Ben .... on his school clothes,
but he ....
breakfast.

3   We put all our school things
     in our school bags.

Ben .... all his
school things in his school bag.

4   We put on our coats and
     say goodbye to our parents.

Ben ....
on his coat and he ....
.... goodbye to his parents.

5   We go out of the house and
     we catch the bus.

Ben .... out of the house but
he .... the bus.

6   We get on the bus.

Ben .... on
the bus.

7   We go into the classroom and
     our teacher is happy with us.

Ben .... into the classroom but
his teacher .... happy.

D ▶ **Complete Nick's story. Write one word on each line.**

I got up and I (1) ...._had_........ a shower. I (2) .... on my clothes
and went downstairs to the kitchen. I had breakfast with my family. Then
I (3) .... my coat from the hall cupboard. I (4) ....
goodbye to my parents and then I (5) .... out of the house.
I walked to the bus stop and I (6) .... the bus to school.
I (7) .... down on the bus and laughed and talked with my friends.
When I (8) .... into the classroom, the teacher (9) ....
very happy because I had all my books and
homework. Ben came into the classroom. He
(10) .... wet. The teacher wasn't happy
with Ben because he didn't have any books or
homework!

E *Funtime* **Play the game! The past verb game.**

75

36 Could you do it?

A Look at the things Sam wanted to do last Saturday. Complete the sentences.

Saturday
- play football with Paul
- do homework
- clean bike
- buy present for Sally
- email Jack and Eva
- go to Sally's party

1 Sam *couldn't play football* with Paul.
2 He .... a present for his friend.
3 He .... Jack and Eva.
4 His bike was dirty but he .... it.
5 He was angry because he ....
   to Sally's party.
6 He .... any homework, but he
   wasn't angry about that!

B ▶ Listen and tick (✔) the box.

1 Where did Sam go
  this afternoon?

 A ☐    B ☐    C ☐

2 What did Sam do
  this morning?

 A ☐    B ☐    C ☐

3 Where is
  Sam's computer?

 A ☐    B ☐    C ☐

4 What homework does
  Sam have to do today?

 A ☐    B ☐    C ☐

5 What number
  is Sally's house?

 A ☐    B ☐    C ☐

C Draw lines from the words to the pictures.

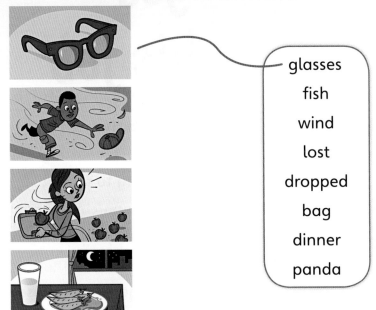

glasses

fish

wind

lost

dropped

bag

dinner

panda

D Choose words from C to complete the sentences.

Example

I couldn't do my homework because my dog hid my
.......glasses....... and I couldn't see.

I couldn't do my homework because ...

① my pet .... ate
my books for ....

② my books fell out of my
school ....

③ the .... was very strong
when I walked home from school.

④ I .... my books
in the river.

⑤ I .... my pen.

E *Funtime* Play the game! Put out the washing!

77

Mr Must changes his job

A Put the words into the circles.

I like ...

I have to ...

have/having a shower

eat/eating breakfas[t]

go/going to school

clean/cleaning my teet[h]

stay/staying in bed

sleep/sleeping

get/getting undressed

watch/watching TV

do/doing homework

play/playing computer games

dry/drying plates

B Read the story and write words to complete the sentences.

Mr Must's exciting letter

Peter Must was a bus driver. He didn't like getting up in the morning but he couldn't stay in bed! Mrs Must woke him up. She said 'Get up, Peter!' After breakfast every morning he had to put on his bus driver's uniform and ride his bike to work in the town centre.

Examples   Mrs Must .... *woke* .... Peter up in the morning.
Mr Must rode .... *his bike* .... to the town centre.

1   Mr Must washed and started the bus, then he had to ....
it round the town all day.

When he got to the bus station, he had to wash the bus. Then he had to start the bus and drive it all day. He had to say 'Good morning!' and smile at the people who got on his bus at every bus stop.

But Mr Must didn't want to be a bus driver. He wanted to work in the countryside.

2   Mr Must said .... to all the people on the bus.
3   Mr Must didn't like being a ....

One evening, when he got home, Mrs Must said, 'A letter came for you today. Here you are!' Mr Must opened his letter and smiled. 'Wow!' he said. 'I don't have to be a bus driver now. We can go and live in the beautiful countryside.' Mrs Must was surprised. 'Can we?' she asked. 'Yes! The letter is from Mr All,' Mr Must answered. 'Listen. Mr All says, "Please come and work for me at Right Farm!"' Mrs Must laughed and said, 'Hooray!'

4   .... gave the letter to Mr Must.
5   Mr and Mrs Must can live in .... now.
6   .... wanted Mr Must to come and work on his farm.
7   Mr Must is happy because he can work at .... !

C Say which picture is different and why.

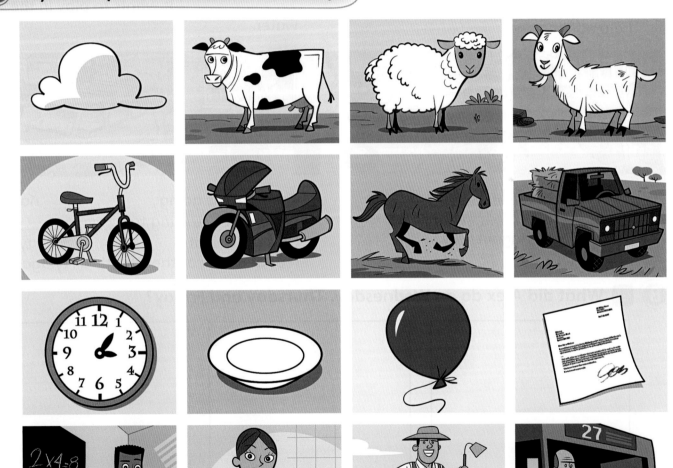

D Talk about how things are different now.

A Complete the sentences to tell the story. You choose the words.

Let's clean the car!

Mr and Mrs .... want to clean their dirty car. Their children .... and .... are helping them.

.... is washing the back of the car. She has a pet. Its name is .... It wants to play in the water.

.... is bringing everyone some .... to drink. The car is .... again now.

The family is going .... now because it's starting to .... Oh no! Look at ....'s dirty feet and look at the car. It's dirty again.

B **What did Alex do on Wednesday, Thursday and Friday?**

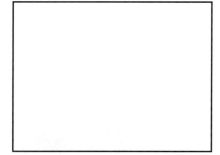

Wednesday

Thursday

Friday

C Talk about the questions.

1 Which was your best day last week? Why was it good?
2 What was the weather like last Wednesday?
3 Who did you help at home at the weekend? How did you help?
4 When did you see your friends? Where did you see them?

D **Read the story. Choose a word from the box.**
Write the correct word next to numbers 1–5.

Grace works at a children's hospital which is in the city ......*centre*...... . She's a
(1) .... Her work changes every week and sometimes, she has to work at
night.

Last Tuesday, Grace slept in the day and woke up in the evening. She cooked
(2) .... and chips for her family's dinner, but Grace only wanted a cup of
coffee! After their dinner, Grace's family watched TV and then went to bed but Grace
had to get into her car and (3) .... to work.

When Grace came home on Wednesday morning, she was really tired and very
(4) .... ! She sat down at the table to have her favourite dinner – pasta!
Her children were at school and the house was quiet. Grace played some music, answered
her emails and text messages then took off her (5) .... and went to bed!

Choose the best name for this story. Tick (✔) one box.

Grace's day at work! ☐   The children's school! ☐   A new car for the family! ☐

Example ✓

centre   sunny   nurse   fish   washed

hungry   clothes   drive   night

E **Find the differences between the pictures.**

39 We've got lots of things to do

A When do you do these things?

1

`08:00`

2

`19:30`

3
`16:00`

4

`23:00`

in the ....   in the ....   in the ....   at ....

Do you ...   write text messages?   clean your teeth?   do your homework?

When do you ...   feed your pet?   have a shower?   play outside?

B Choose the correct words and write them on the lines.

Is it **easy, difficult, boring** or **exciting** to be a farmer?

Example	Farmer Jack is 90 now. He likes telling school children about when he .... *was* .... young. 'I always got up at four o'clock. I had a quick wash and a quick breakfast, then I went to see the cows in my fields.		was	is	wer
1	At about seven o'clock I .... back home on my tractor and had my second breakfast.	1	comes	came	com
2	I worked .... the morning, the afternoon and the evening.	2	on	by	in
3	When .... was something wrong with one of the animals, I sometimes had to get up	3	there	it	she
4	.... night and work hard then, too.	4	at	after	to
5	I worked .... day in all kinds of weather. I could never take a break or have a holiday but I didn't always work on Sunday evenings!'	5	many	every	som

C Draw lines between the question and the answer.

Do you ...

clean the bath?

cook the dinner?

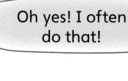

Oh yes! I often do that!

I do, sometimes!

No, never!

Yes, every day!

I always do that!

wash your clothes?

make your bed?

Do you carry .... ?   Do you work .... ?

Do you tidy .... ?   Do you paint .... ?

D ▶ Listen and write.

MILBROOK
Sports Centre

Homework

Teacher's name: Charlie ......*Smith*......

1 Age: ....

2 Day gives tennis lessons: on ....

3 When / Charlie's lessons: in the ....

4 Number of children in class: ....

5 Charlie wants to teach: ...., too.

E What about you? Complete the sentences.

1 On Monday morning, I always ....

2 In the afternoon at school, we often ....

3 In the evening, I sometimes ....

4 I never .... on Sunday night.

40 People who help us

A Write 1, 2 or 3 words to complete the sentences about the story.

Lost in the forest!

On Sunday, Jim and Paul went to a lake with their parents. The boys and their puppy, Tiger, played on some grass next to the forest there. Paul threw a yellow ball. Tiger ran to find it in the forest, but he didn't come back again.

Examples   Jim's family went to .... *a lake* .... on Sunday.
Tiger is the boys' .... *puppy* ....

1   Tiger didn't come back when the boys played on
.... near the forest.

The boys looked for Tiger in the forest but they couldn't find him. 'We must ask someone to help us,' Jim said. 'Look! There's a police car. Quickly, Dad! Stop it!'

The car stopped and a police officer got out. 'What's the matter?' he asked. The family told him all about Tiger. 'I can help!' he said. 'Let's look by the lake again and behind the trees, too.'

2   A .... came to help the family find their pet.
3   Everyone looked for the puppy .... and by the lake.

Paul and the police officer found something in the middle of some leaves. 'It's Tiger's yellow ball!' Paul said. And what's that noise?' Jim asked. 'Listen! By that tree? Something's black, and look, it's moving!' 'It's Tiger's tail!' laughed the police officer.

Paul ran to pick Tiger up. 'Naughty dog!' he said and laughed. Tiger jumped out of his arms and ran to the ball. 'I think he wants to play another game!' the police officer smiled. 'But I must go back to work. Have a great afternoon! And Tiger, don't get lost again!'

4   They found Tiger's ball and then .... saw something black near a tree.
5   Paul picked Tiger up but he .... his arms.
6   Tiger wanted to play ....
7   The police officer told Tiger not to .... again!

Example Missing pet: puppy.................................

1 When lost: this ....

2 Boy's name: Jim ....

3 Boy's address: .... City Road

4 Where pet lost: near the ....

5 Colour of pet: black, white and ....

C **Listen and say.**

The boys **looked** for their lost puppy!

D **Complete the conversation about your pet.**

What's the matter?

I can't find my ....

Police officer: When did you lose your * .... ?
You: I lost it ....

Police officer: And what's your name?
You: It's ....

Police officer: Where were you when you lost your * .... ?
You: I was ....

Police officer: Tell me more about your * .... ?
You: OK. It's ....

E Funtime **Play the game.**

F **My work day!**

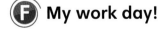

41 I had a great birthday

(A) Complete sentences about the picture. Write names and draw lines.

1   Two people have got numbers on .... *their clothes* ....
2   The girl in the pink dress isn't wearing ....
3   A man with the camera is ....
4   Above the presents, you can see ....
5   Two of the people in the band are ....
6   On the table, there are lots of ....

...*Lucy*...

....

....

....

....

....

....

....

....

(B) Read and choose the best answer.

1   **Alex:** Hello Lucy! It was your birthday yesterday. Happy birthday!
   Lucy: A   Don't worry!
          B   Me too!
          (C) Thanks!

2   **Alex:** Did you enjoy your party?
   Lucy: A   Yes, it was great!
          B   Yes, I can come today.
          C   Yes, there were two.

3   **Alex:** What did you do at the party?
   Lucy: A   Is it a computer mouse?
          B   You can practise that dance.
          C   We played games and had fun.

4   **Alex:** Did your mum make a cake?
   Lucy: A   No, my aunt made it.
          B   My mother's called Daisy.
          C   Put it on the table, please.

5   **Alex:** How many people were at your party?
   Lucy: A   What a nice day!
          B   I don't know. Lots!
          C   It was really cool!

C **Read the story. Choose a word from the box.**
Write the correct word next to numbers 1–5.

It was my .....birthday..... last weekend. My parents took my sister and me
to Forest Farm. Forest Farm is a kind of (1)....................... where you can see
and play with lots of different animals. You can watch dogs that work with
animals like (2)....................... and goats. I helped the grown-ups to give
the chickens their breakfast and my sister took some brilliant photos of two
donkeys. Then we had something to eat in the farm café. I had some cheese
and tomato sandwiches and Mum (3)....................... my sister sausages with
tomato sauce and fries. Her favourite! After lunch, Dad took us down to a
kind of basement which had a red door. 'Now (4)....................... your eyes,
Jack,' he said. I did! He opened the door. 'You can look now' he laughed.
Everyone in my class was there! I was really (5)....................... ! We played
lots of funny games. It was a fantastic party and a very exciting day!

Example

birthday	bought	zoo
sheep	windy	close
lunch	surprised	hid

Choose the best name for the story. Tick (✔) one box.

Dad's favourite pet ☐   A great day at the farm ☐
Mum makes a cake ☐

D **Find the presents and draw lines.**

1   I'm pretty and you wear me round your neck.
2   I can dry you after a bath!
3   You must cook us!
4   Sit on my seat and ride me to school!
5   I'm brown and sweet to eat.

E **Funtime** **Play the game! Birthday presents.**

F **Plan your party!**

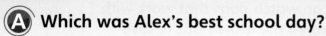

42 An exciting week for Alex

A **Which was Alex's best school day?**

Friday was good. It was more exciting than Thursday.

Monday was worse than Tuesday.

I enjoyed Thursday more than Tuesday.

I thought Tuesday wasn't bad ...

Wednesday was better then Friday.

B ▶ **Listen to Alex telling her grandfather about her week. Where did Alex go with each of these people? Listen and write a letter in each box.**

her aunt	her uncle	her classmates	her cousin	her dad	her mum
F	☐	☐	☐	☐	☐

A  B  C  D

E  F  G  H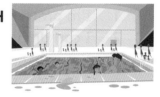

C **A day in the city.**  PROJECT

D **Charlie's going to the zoo. Listen and draw circles around his correct answers.**

Dad:	Would you like to take something to eat?
Charlie:	Yes, please, Dad! So do I!
Dad:	Well, here's a milkshake and some chicken and salad sandwiches.
Charlie:	Cool! Excuse me!
Dad:	How about taking some orange juice, too?
Charlie:	There they are! Good idea!
Dad:	What about some of Grandma's coffee cake?
Charlie:	I'm good at that. All right!
Dad:	And would you like to buy an ice cream at the zoo?
Charlie:	How are you? No, thanks!
Dad:	And have you got your ticket, Charlie?
Charlie:	Yes. Don't worry! Hooray!

E **Find the differences between the pictures.**

F **Funtime Play the game! Say thanks.**

43 My holidays

A Let's talk about holidays.

1 Do you enjoy going on holiday?
2 What do you like eating on holiday?
3 Who do you go on holiday with?
4 What do you like doing on holiday?

a My grandparents.
b Yes, it's great.
c At the beach.
d Playing tennis.
e Coffee ice cream.

Tell me about your last holiday.

B Read and choose the best answer.

1 **Mr Ride:** Did you enjoy your holiday, Jill?

   Jill: A Last year.
         B All right!
         C Yes, thanks!

2 **Mr Ride:** Where did you go?
   Jill: A We sat in a circle.
         B To the jungle.
         C Yes, I'm going to bed.

3 **Mr Ride:** How did you get there?
   Jill: A Bring your bike!
         B I'm crossing the road.
         C We went by helicopter.

4 **Mr Ride:** What sport did you do on your holiday?
   Jill: A We went swimming.
         B It's a tennis racket.
         C I don't know the score.

5 **Jill:** Here are two photos!
   Mr Ride: A On my laptop.
         B Wow! They're great!
         C Excuse me, Jill!

C Find the differences between the pictures.

D Read Fred's story. Write the correct word next to the numbers.

My holiday by Fred Top

My name's Fred and I ....love........ going on holiday. For our holiday last year, we went to an island. We travelled there by [(1)] .... That was exciting too!

It was hot and [(2)] .... every day on the island, but sometimes it rained a lot at night.

The food there was fantastic. We ate a lot of [(3)] .... , kiwis and fish and one day, Dad cooked pancakes for us which we had with lemon sauce! We went for long walks along the beach and on our last day, I saw some jellyfish! Mum thought they were scary, but I loved them. I took my [(4)] .... to take photos of everything and play games on and I brought back some really pretty shells. I gave the best one to my [(5)] .... She loved it.

sunny   ~~love~~   tablet   plane
clever   pineapples   climb   grandma

E Complete sentences about two dream holidays!

	mine	yours
I'd love to go to	....	....
I'd love to travel there by	....	....
I'd love to go there with	....	....
On my dream holiday, I'd love to	.... and and .... !	.... and and .... !

F Answer questions! What an exciting trip!

G An island project.

PROJECT

44 Along the beach

The wet T-shirts. Look at the pictures. Tell the story.

1

Nick   Sam

2

3

4

B **Complete the sentences about the story. Write 1, 2 or 3 words.**

The wet T-shirts!

Last Tuesday, Sam and his brother Nick went for a long walk along the beach.
They put their towels and clothes down in their favourite place on the sand and then
played football. Then they ran and jumped into the waves.

Examples   Nick has a ......_brother_...... called Sam.
Before their game of football, the boys had a walk ......_along the beach_...... .

1   After their game, the boys .... into the sea.

The boys swam under the water to look for shells and sea animals. Then they swam
around some big rocks and, when they were tired, climbed up out of the water and
sat on them to watch the sailing boats. Then Nick saw something orange in the water
by their feet. He picked it up and said, 'Look! It's your orange T-shirt, Sam! You put it
too near the sea!'

2   Nick and Sam wanted to find some .... under the water.
3   Then the boys sat on a rock to watch ....
4   Nick saw Sam's .... in the sea.

Then Nick saw his green T-shirt in the sea, too and said, 'Quick, Sam! Get it for me!'

The brothers swam back to the beach with their wet T-shirts. When they got there,
only one of their shoes was on the sand. 'We put those too near the sea, too,'
Sam said.

They walked to the bus stop in their wet clothes and then caught a bus home. When
they told their parents everything, Mum said, 'You must be more careful!' 'But we're
happy that you're both safe!' Dad added.

5   The boys lost three of their .... in the water.
6   Nick and Sam stood by a .... to wait for their bus.
7   Their parents were happy because the boys were ....

C **Read the sentences and find the answers in the story.**

1   After a swim, you can dry your body with these.   ....*towels*.........
2   Swimsuits, shorts and skirts are examples of these.   ....
3   This is under your feet when you walk on a beach.   ....
4   You can climb up or on to these. They're often grey.   ....
5   You need a ticket to travel on this in town.   a ....
6   These people are your mother and your father.   ....

D **Read the sentences. Write words which mean the same.**

1   take something off the floor   p__ __ __ something u__
2   have a swim or a walk   g__ f__ __   a swim or a walk
3   take a bus   c__ __ __ __   a bus
4   email   s__ __ __   an email
5   put on your clothes   g__ __   d__ __ __ __ __ __
6   go to the shops   g__   s__ __ __ __ __ __ __

E **Find ten more pairs! Draw lines.**

write   I   pair   read   son   aunt

wear   red   sun   for   eye   where

eight   know   sea   see   no   right

aren't   four   ate   pear

F **Find the differences between the pictures.**

1

2

G **Funtime** Play the game! Let's find A–Z.

45 Treasure!

A Look and read. Choose the correct words and write them on the lines.

a ticket   maps   treasure   islands

a pirate   a bee   the sky   a ship

Example   This person is in stories and sometimes he has a parrot! ....a pirate.......
1   You have to buy this when you go to watch a film. ....
2   You see the sun in this in the day and the moon at night. ....
3   You look at these to find roads to different towns. ....
4   These places have water all round them. ....
5   Pirates look for this under the water or under the ground. ....
6   Some people travel on this when they need to cross the sea. ....

B Colour the words you can make from the name of the film!

Pirates and Parrots

| tests | parents | apps | seats | trousers | parties | sisters | dinner | pandas |

C Write 1, 2 or 3 words to complete the sentences about the story.

Last week, my parents and I read about a film on the internet. We bought the tickets and went to see it at the *Star Cinema* on Sunday. The film was about a famous pirate called Dan. He wore black boots and had a black beard and moustache. He had a parrot too, whose name was Clever. Clever always sat on Dan's shoulder.

Examples   The boy and his ......*parents*...... read about the film on the internet.
On Sunday, they went to see the film at ..*the Star Cinema*.. .

1   There was .... in the film whose name was Dan.
2   Clever was Dan's ....

In the film, Dan and his pirates sailed to a small island. When they got
to the beach, Dan was hot and tired. 'Find something for us all to eat!'
he said to the pirates. 'Something for Clever too!' Dan's pirates found
lots of bananas, pineapples, coconuts and kiwis to eat. They sat down
in a circle on the sand, ate and then went to sleep after all their work.

3   The pirates went to a .... in their ship.
4   Dan told the pirates to .... some food for everyone.
5   The pirates all had something to eat, then they
.... on the beach.

Then Clever made a really loud noise and Dan and the pirates woke
up. Clever jumped up and down and said, 'Pretty treasure! Pretty
treasure!' 'Clever's never wrong. There's treasure here!' Dan said.
The pirates found the box under the sand and laughed very loudly
when they looked inside. That night the moon in the sky looked
beautiful and all the pirates sang and danced and played music on
the sand. I loved the film. It was fantastic.

6   Dan knew that there was some .... under the sand
because Clever was always right!
7   When the pirates found the treasure, they .... on the beach
under the beautiful moon.

D **Talk about differences between pictures 2 and 3.**

E **Let's write five-line poems!**

46 A day on the island

A ▶ **Listen and draw lines.**

Sam   Peter   Vicky   Grace

Sally   Alex   Jack

B **Look and read and write.**

Examples   The pirate on the ship is wearing .... *a black hat* ....
            What is the person in the small boat doing?   .... *fishing* ....

Complete the sentences. Write 1, 2, 3, 4 or 5 words.

1   The woman in the pink dress has got ....
2   A parrot is sitting at the top of ....

Answer the questions. Write 1, 2, 3, 4 or 5 words.

3   What is the man in the orange shorts holding?   ....
4   Where is the girl hiding?   ....

Now write two sentences about the picture.

5   ....
6   ....

C **Listen and say.**

The **pirate** in the **big boat** has a **black hat** on his **head!**

E Listen, write the words, questions and answers.

?

?

?

?

F Write your question and yes or no answer.

Question ....?
Answer: ....

G Funtime Play the game! Guess my question.

97

47 The different things we do

A Things I do. Draw lines.

1 answer   a my pet rabbit
2 wait at   b my phone
3 invite   c up in funny clothes
4 water   d a model plane
5 build   e to sleep
6 dress   f my friends to a party
7 clap   g the bus stop
8 go   h my hands
9 feed   i from 1 to 100
10 count   j my mum's favourite plant

B Listen and tick (✔) the box.

1 What is Peter doing now?

A ☐   B ☐   C ☐

2 What is Jane doing now?

A ☐   B ☐   C ☐

3 What is Paul doing now?

A ☐   B ☐   C ☐

4 What is Alex doing now?

A ☐   B ☐   C ☐

C Draw a circle round the word that means the same thing!

lift   eara__he   elevator   everyone
shop   store   sp__rt   skate
film   moon   moustac__e   movie
football   son   __occer   soup
sweets   candy   centre   c__untry
flat   a__phabet   armchair   apartment

Now make a word with the missing letters! ....

 98

D ▶ **Listen and colour and write.**

....

....

E **Who is doing what? Write names and complete the sentences.**

1 .... and .... are w..................... !
2 .... is s..................... on a seat.
3 .... is j..................... into the water.
4 .... is w..................... a T-shirt.
5 .... is s..................... in the pool.

F **Say 'Yes, that's right' or 'No that's wrong'!**

G **Funtime Play a game! Change places or Mime the words!**

48 We want to do this one day

A What are your answers? One day, would you like to ... ?

1

2

3

4

5

6

7

8

B Read and choose the best answer.

Example

Tom: Hello, Zoe. What are you reading about?

Zoe: A Along the beach.
   (B) A really cool woman.
   C I can't practise today.

Questions

1 Tom: What did the woman do?
   Zoe: A She sailed around the world.
      B That's her funny story!
      C She's not by the beach.

2 Tom: When did you start reading this book?
   Zoe: A Every day.
      B In my room.
      C Last weekend.

3 Tom: Who gave you the book?
   Zoe: A No, it's my sister's.
      B Is it hers or his?
      C My dad bought it.

4 Tom: Do you like the book?
   Zoe: A Yes, you are.
      B Yes, it is.
      C Yes, I do.

5 Tom: Is it a very long book?
   Zoe: A There aren't many pages.
      B I'm sorry about that.
      C I'm not silly.

6 Tom: Can I read the book after you?
   Zoe: A Don't worry!
      B Yes, OK!
      C So do I!

Read the story. Choose a word from the box. Write the correct word next to numbers 1–5.

Last Tuesday, Zoe's father bought his daughter a present from the new bookshop in the town centre. It was a story that Zoe wanted to read about a ......_woman_...... who sailed round the world in a very small boat. Her name was Mary Banks and she was only 22. It was a very exciting story. Sometimes the waves were really big and the wind was very strong. She saw jellyfish, (1)...................... and sharks in the sea. She was often (2)...................... but she was never frightened. When Mary came home, lots of people wanted to read about her.

There was a website about Mary's trip around the world and an e-book. There was a story about her on the back (3)...................... of Zoe's favourite comic too! Zoe loved reading about Mary. 'Can we (4)...................... a boat, Dad?' she asked. 'I want to sail around the world, too!' Zoe's father smiled. 'I think that's a great idea, Zoe. But first you must learn to (5)......................!'

Example

woman	tired	downstairs
raining	buy	whales
swim	page	tablet

Choose the best name for the story. Tick (✔) one box.

Dad's new boat   ☐

Learning about Mary   ☐

Zoe's sailing lesson   ☐

D **Write a story about a story! Choose words.**

E **Let's see! How well do you know your friend?**

A Make sentences with these words.

1 **Miss Page:** this? / What's

....
What's this?
....

2 **Sam:** don't / I / Sorry, / know

....

Miss Page: It's a helicopter.

3 **Sam:** please? / again / you / Can / say / that

....

Miss Page: It's a helicopter.

4 **Sam:** do / How / spell / you / helicopter ?

....

Miss Page: H–E–L–I–C–O–P–T–E–R.

Sam: H–E–L–I–C–O–P–T–E–R. OK! Thank you.

B Talk about the picture.

C Where are these things things in the picture? Draw lines.

The coat is	in the cupboard.
The fish is	in the bowl.
The helicopter is	on the handbag.
The rainbow is	above the sea.
The mouse is	behind the woman's head.
The dolphin is	below the clock.
The map of the world is	next to the window.

D Answer questions and draw pictures.

What was the weather like yesterday?

It was ....

What's the weather like today?

It's .... and ....

What's the teacher's school bag like?

It's .... and it's got a
.... on it.

What's your school bag like?

It's .... and it's got
....

E Read and choose the best answer.

Example

Mrs Pat: Hello, Sue.
Sue:
   A   Good morning!
   B   Thank you!
   C   Well done!

1   Mrs Pat: How old are you, Sue?
    Sue:
     A   Fine, thanks.
     B   I'm ten.
     C   Sue Young.

2   Mrs Pat: Who do you play with?
    Sue:
     A   In the playground.
     B   At the end of school.
     C   The kids in my class.

3   Mrs Pat: What sports do you play?
    Sue:
     A   My tennis racket.
     B   Baseball and skateboarding.
     C   My best friend's bat.

4   Mrs Pat: Have you got a pet?
    Sue:
     A   Snails are so funny!
     B   No, but I'd like a penguin!
     C   Brown bears are scary!

5   Mrs Pat: And what's your favourite food?
    Sue:
     A   Apple pie, I think.
     B   They aren't meatballs.
     C   I drew a milkshake.

F Choose answers and questions!

G Listen and answer!

A Say what you see in the pictures.
Find words that sound the same.

B ▶ Listen and tick (✔) the box.

Example: Which is Daisy?

A ☐ B ☐ C ☐

1 What does Kim need?

A ☐ B ☐ C ☐

2 Where is Tony now?

A ☐ B ☐ C ☐

3 What is on Ben's computer screen?

A ☐ B ☐ C ☐

4 What did Pat do in his test?

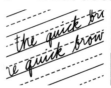 

A ☐ B ☐ C ☐

5 What does Jim want to do now?

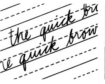

A ☐ B ☐ C ☐

C Play the game! Stepping stones.

the end

z you see animals here

y not today

5 things you can see in the country

t 4 places in a town

u not bottom

not downstairs

v smaller than a town

w not better

s not weak

r not square

q not loud

p children play here

3 places with water

o not closed

n not good

k a room in a house

j another place with trees

l not first

m you climb this

i not outside

h not cold

g not terrible

f a place with trees

e not boring

d not clean

c not straight

b not ugly

the start

a not before

2   Animals, animals ...

1   Crocodiles eat fish, birds, animals and sometimes they eat people too! They do not eat grass or plants.
2   A crocodile has a long body and mouth and a long tail. A crocodile has short legs. But be careful because they can swim and they can run too!
3   A mother crocodile sits on her eggs for about 12 weeks then the eggs open. The mother carries her baby crocodiles into the river.
4   You can find crocodiles in many parts of the world. Some crocodiles only live in rivers but some crocodiles can live in the sea too.
5   When crocodiles swim they can see. Their mouths are under the water but their eyes are above the water. A crocodile's eyes are on the top of its head.
6   Look inside a crocodile's mouth and you can find a lot of teeth! They can have between 60 and 80 teeth. People have about 30 teeth.
7   Crocodiles are dangerous animals. You should never go near them!

5   The woman in the red dress

Learner A
Let's talk about the clothes you wear.
1   What clothes would you like to buy?
2   What do you wear when it's wet?
3   What **don't** you wear when it's cold?
4   What do you wear at home?
5   Where do you put your clothes at night?

9   Me and my family

Learner A
Now let's talk about you and your family.
1   How many people are there in your family?
2   Does your family live in a house or in a flat?
3   What do you do with your family at weekends?
4   Tell me about the youngest person in your family.

26 Guess who lives here?

11 Things we eat and drink

Learner A
Let's talk about you and food.

1 Who buys your food?
2 Where does your family buy their food?
3 What do you have for breakfast?
4 What vegetables do you like?
5 Who is the best cook in your family?

Now find words inside the words!

meatballs
sandwich
orange

5   The woman in the red dress

Learner B

Let's talk about the clothes you wear.
1   Where do you get dressed?
2   What colour are your favourite clothes?
3   What clothes are you wearing now?
4   What clothes **don't** you wear when it's hot?
5   What's the **last thing** you put on in the morning?

9   Me and my family

Learner B

Now let's talk about you and your family.
1   How many cousins have you got?
2   Does your family live by the sea or in a town?
3   Where do you go with your family on holiday?
4   Tell me about the oldest person in your family.

11   Things we eat and drink

Learner B

Let's talk about you and food.
1   Who cooks the meals in your house?
2   Where do you have lunch?
3   Do you help in the kitchen at home?
4   What fruit don't you like?
5   What is your favourite dinner?

Now find words inside the words!
mango
pancake
candy

20 Where?

Learner A: Colour the biggest mountain blue, the boy's hair brown, the girl's bag pink, the trees on the left green, the rock behind the boy grey.

21 Here and there in town

Learner A
Let's talk about your town.
Where do you like going on Saturdays?
What do you do there?
Who do you go there with?
Tell me about your favourite place in town.

20 Where?

Learner B: Colour the boy's bag purple, the girl's jacket yellow, the smallest duck on the right orange, the trees on the right red.

21 Here and there in town

Learner B
Let's talk about your town.
Where does your family buy your food?
How do you go there?
When do you go there?
Tell me about your favourite place in town.

Seeing differences

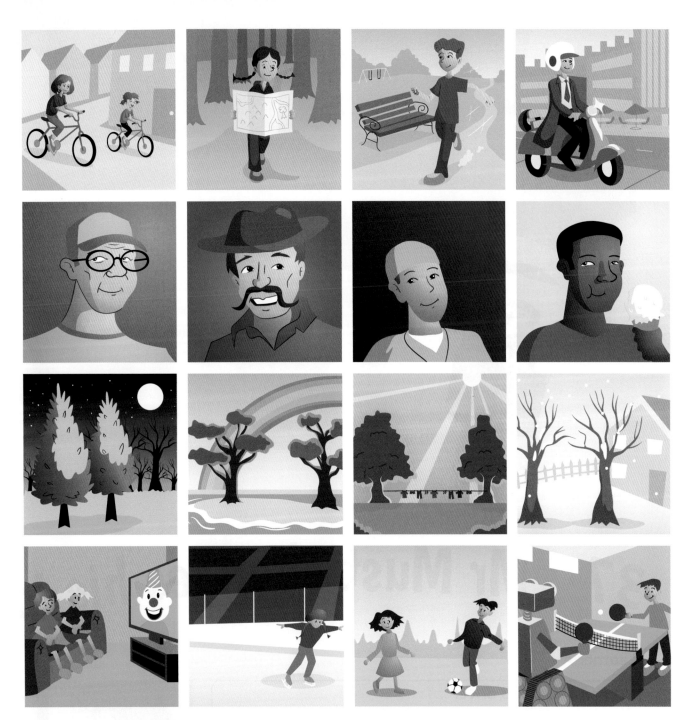

Talk about these questions:

1 Do you like hopping games? Why / why not?

2 Do children at your school skip in the playground? What's your favourite playground game? How do you play it?

3 What games do you play when you're home? Who do you play with?

4 What kind of weather is good for skating? Have you got a pair of roller skates or ice skates?

5 Does anyone that you know have to wear a hat or helmet at work? What's their job? Why do they have to wear a hat or helmet?

28 Our busy holidays

37 Mr Must changes his job

Learner A

When I was a bus driver ...
I had to .... a uniform.
I .... to say 'Good morning' to everyone who got on my bus.
I had to .... the dirty bus.
I couldn't .... in bed because I had to get up!
I couldn't have any pets because we .... in a small flat.

16

38 Playing and working

Learner A
Ben's week

	Monday	Tuesday	Wednesday	Thursday	Friday
Morning					
Afternoon					
Evening					

43 My holidays

Answer questions.

What an exciting trip!

When did you go on your trip?

....

Where did you go?

....

Who did you go there with?

....

How did you get there?

....

What did you do first when you got there?

....

Which part of the trip was really exciting?

....

Would you like to go on a trip like this again?

....

37 Mr Must changes his job

Learner B

Now, because I work on a farm
I can't stay in bed but I like getting up because I .... my job!
I have to .... the tractor and farm truck when they're dirty.
I can .... lots of pets!
I can .... the clothes that I like!
I can .... 'Hello' to the farm animals!

38 Playing and working

Learner B
Anna's week

	Monday	Tuesday	Wednesday	Thursday	Friday
Morning		reading			
Afternoon	running		listening to music		shopping
Evening				TV	

34   What did you do then?

Find five differences between the pictures.

1

2

40   People who help us

This driver lives in ....

This driver gets up at .... o'clock.

This driver has .... for breakfast.

This driver takes a .... with them to work.

This driver drives to .... at eleven o'clock.

At one o'clock, this driver stops work and walks to the
....

This driver phones their ....

This driver has .... for lunch.

This driver starts work again at ....

There are lots of .... in this driver's lorry /
truck / bus.

Sometimes, this driver has to drive to ....

At five o'clock, this driver is ....

This driver goes home and ....

This driver really .... their job!

115

Unit wordlist

1
places
playground

verbs
climb
dance
hop
jump
move
run
roller skate
skip
talk
walk
watch

adjectives
good at

adverbs
all day
round

2
animals
baby
bat
bear
bee
bird
cage
cat
cow
crocodile
dog
dolphin
donkey
fish
fly
frog
goat

jellyfish
kangaroo
lion
lizard
monkey
mouse/mice
panda
parrot
penguin
polar bear
rabbit
shark
snail
tail
whale
zebra
zoo

verbs
sound like

prepositions
about (12 weeks)

3
animals
chicken
duck
kitten
pet
puppy
sheep

places
farm
field

transport
tractor
truck

verbs
be called
carry

feed
help
would like

adjectives
frightened of
sweet

4
body and face
beard
eye
face
hair
moustache

people
alien
film star

other nouns
line

colours
black
blue
brown
gray
green
grey
orange
purple
red
white

verbs
change
look in the mirror
paint

adjectives
blond/blonde
cool
curly

fair
long
scary
short
straight
ugly

5
clothes
baseball cap
boot
coat
dress
hat
helmet
jacket
jeans
pair
scarf
shirt
shoe
shorts
skirt
sock
sweater
swimsuit
trousers
T-shirt

things
bag
glasses

verbs
get dressed
put on
wear

prepositions
behind
into
next to

6

body and face
arm
back
ear
foot
hand
head
leg
mouth
neck
nose
shoulder
stomach
tooth/teeth

sports and leisure
monster
player
robot

animals
wing

verbs
go home
hold

7

weather
cloud
rain
rainbow
snow
weather
wind

the world around us
moon
sky
star
sun

leisure
painting
painting class

verbs
draw
fly a kite
get wet
rain
snow

adjectives
cloudy
cold
double
fantastic
hot
sunny
windy

expressions
Oh dear!
Well done!
What's ... like?
Wow!

8

animals
elephant
fur
giraffe
hippo
snake

weather
ice
kind of weather

the world around us
part of the world

verbs
get cold
go to bed
sleep
wake up

adjectives
clever
dry
naughty
strong

tall
wet

adverbs
today
yesterday

9

family
aunt
brother
cousin
dad
daughter
father
granddaughter
grandfather
grandma
grandpa
grandparent
grandson
mother
mum
parent
sister
son
uncle

verbs
answer
ask
call (name)
make a noise

adjectives
busy
loud
old
quiet
silly
young

prepositions
around

expressions
Good idea!

10

people
sports teacher

daily life
phone number

school
paper
tablet

verbs
cook
give music lessons
invite
stop
wait
wash

adjectives
huge
little
nice

expressions
Here you are.
I don't know.
So do I.

11

fruit
apple
banana
coconut
fruit
grape
kiwi
lemon
lime
mango
orange
pear
pineapple
watermelon

meat
burger
chicken

meatball
sausage

vegetables
bean
carrot
onion
pea
potato

drinks
coffee
drink
juice
lemonade
milk
milkshake
tea
water

food
bread
candy
cheese
chips
chocolate
egg
fish
fries
ice cream
noodles
pancake
pasta
pie
rice
salad
sandwich
sauce
soup
sugar
sweet

verbs
grow
make
plant

12
food and drink
bottle
bowl
box
cup
glass
plate

birthday
balloon
birthday
party
present

the home
CD player
cupboard
shelf
table

sport
baseball
bat

verbs
add

adjectives
big
round
square

adverbs
inside
outside

expressions
Brilliant!

shapes
shape

13
the home
balcony
basement
bookcase
chimney

flower
front door
garden
grass
hall
home
leaf
mat
roof
stairs
wall
window

leisure
cameraman
film
movie
video

verbs
have a wash

adjectives
brave
closed
exciting
famous
fun
open

adverbs
downstairs
upstairs

prepositions
above
below
in front of
inside
on
outside

expressions
Come on!
Hi!
Hooray!
How exciting!

Really?
Sorry.

14
the home
address
apartment
bathroom
bedroom
dining room
flat
ground floor
house
kitchen
lift
living room
room

shapes
circle
pentagon
rectangle
square
triangle

adjectives
dark
light

adverbs
downstairs
upstairs

prepositions
near

15
leisure
guitar
music
piano

school
answer
board
classmate
classroom
computer mouse

cross
desk
homework
keyboard
lesson
listening
map
page
pencil
picture
poster
question
reading
rubber
ruler
speaking
test
tick
writing

people
kids

time
o'clock

verbs
make a mistake
play music
point
talk

adjectives
correct
right
wrong

16
sports and leisure
badminton
ball game
basketball
bat
dance
fishing
football
game

hockey
horse riding
ice skate
ice skating
net
player
sailing
skating
soccer
sports centre
table tennis
tennis
TV

verbs
hit
kick
laugh
play (football)
shout
swim
throw
watch

adjectives
boring
favourite
fun
funny
great
OK

expressions
Cool!
Help!

other nouns
favourite

17
sports and leisure
comic
comic book
dancing
drawing
DVD
hobby

radio
story
swimming

beach
beach
rock
sand
sea
towel

verbs
bounce
enjoy
go to sleep
like
love
wave

18
health
doctor
hospital
nurse
temperature

places
building
seat

work
dentist
driver

verbs
have a temperature
practise
take your
   temperature

adjectives
asleep
bad
careful
hungry
ill
sick
terrible

tired
well

pronouns
where
who
that

19
health
backache
cold
cough
dentist
earache
headache
stomach-ache
toothache

people
boy
girl
man
woman

verbs
fix
hurt

adjectives
all right
awake
fine

sports and leisure
practice

expressions
Don't worry!
What's the matter?

20
places
car park
funfair
market
supermarket

the home
rug

food and drink
picnic

other nouns
noise

verbs
buy
get better
go for a bike ride
have a picnic

adjectives
afraid
thirsty

21
places
café
cinema
circus
library
park
station
sweet shop
town

work
clown

the home
chair

**the world
around us**
wave

animals
tiger

transport
postcard
ticket

clothes
handbag

verbs
catch a bus
choose
go for a swim

have a drink
have lunch
see a doctor

adverbs
here
there

questions
What?
Where?
Who?

expressions
I've got to go!
See you!

22
places
bookshop
bus stop
city
road
shopping centre
shop window
street
village

numbers
hundred
thousand

sports and leisure
racket

transport
motorbike

the home
poster

verbs
go for a boat ride
know
think

23
**the world
around us**
country
country(side)

forest
island
jungle
lake
mountain
river
waterfall
world

places
car park

adjectives
dangerous
high

prepositions
down
up

determiners
many

conjunctions
because
or

questions
How much?

24
technology
app
e-book
email
(the) internet
message
photo
text
video
website

school
alphabet
letter

other nouns
difference
thing

verbs
add photos
call
get a message
make a video
phone
send
take pictures
text

adverbs
only

pronouns
everyone
some

25
the home
armchair
sofa
toothbrush
toothpaste

work
cook
pop star

verbs
cry
learn
ride a horse
say yes
want

adjectives
beautiful
different
pretty
small
ugly

conjunctions
but

26
the home
CD
lamp

animals
spider

sports and leisure
skateboarding

verbs
come home
drive to work
move into a flat
water

prepositions
after
before
between
from
opposite
out of
round

prepositional phrases
at home
at the back of
at the bottom of
at the end
at the top of
on top of

27
leisure
band
laptop

work
at work
job

other nouns
idea

verbs
find
go for a walk
have a dream
put
run a lot
see

watch a video
write a song

adjectives
asleep
naughty

28
people
best friend
wife

transport
a balloon ride
helicopter

time
school holiday

verbs
fish
go running
go sailing
go shopping
go swimming
hide
make a cake
teach

adverbs
always
never
often

determiner
every

questions
How often?

29
toys
doll

verbs
clap
clean your teeth
count
drop
fall asleep

learn English
wave goodbye

adjectives
surprised

adverbs
badly
carefully
loudly
quickly
quietly
sadly
slowly
very
well

30
people
grown-up

school
art
marks
maths
spelling

verbs
go away on holiday
Let's talk
listen to music
sing songs
test
use a keyboard

questions
How?
How many?
How old?

When?
Which?
Why?

expressions
bye
goodbye

31
the home
bath
blanket
shower

toys
teddy bear

verbs
cry
have a shower
need

adjectives
angry
clean
dirty
happy
new
sad

determiner
another

32
food
kilo
tomato

verbs
understand

adjectives
angry
empty
safe

adverbs
first
then

prepositions
along
behind

pronouns
everything
nothing

determiners
all
a little
a lot of
not many
not much
some

expressions
Thank you.
try looking

33
time
Friday
Monday
Saturday
Sunday
Thursday
Tuesday
Wednesday
watch
week
weekend

places
pool
swimming pool

sports and leisure
crayon
skateboard

verbs
give someone a
  present

adjectives
last

34
transport
kilometre
ship

sports and leisure
board game

verbs
colour a picture
dress up
find
give someone a
  present
open a present
plant
put on
show
start to rain
stop playing
talk about

adverbs
now

35
school
school things

transport
bus stop
place

food
breakfast
dinner
lunch

time
diary

verbs
get off the bus
get on the bus
get to school
get up
go to bed
wake up

adjectives
late

adverbs
late

36
school
pen

verbs
clean
could
do your homework
fall out of your bag
invite someone for
  dinner
lose

questions
Whose?

37
places
bus station
town centre

work
bus driver
uniform

home
CD
clock
toy

verbs
drive a bus
dry
get undressed
have to
smile
start the bus
stay in bed

expressions
Good morning
Hello

38
time
afternoon
day
evening
morning
night

places
children's hospital
city centre

verbs
answer emails
take off (clothes)

39
people
age
name

verbs
cook the dinner
give food to a pet
have a holiday
have a quick
  breakfast
have a quick wash
make your bed
take a break
tell someone about
work hard
write a text message

adjectives
difficult
easy
something wrong

adverbs
sometimes

40
transport
lorry

work
driver
police car
police officer

verbs
come back
get lost
look for
lose
must

adjectives
missing

adverbs
again

determiners
another

pronouns
someone
something

questions
What's the matter?

41
toys
model

verbs
close
film
play the piano

pronouns
lots

expressions
Excuse me.
Happy birthday!
How about …?
Me too!
What about …?
No, thanks.
Thanks!
Yes, please.

42
verbs
make friends with
take someone on a
  trip

adjectives
best
better
more exciting
worse
worst

expressions
All right!

43
transport
plane

sports and leisure
camera
dream holiday
score

**the world
around us**
shell

time
last year

verbs
bring
cross the road
go on holiday
sit in a circle
travel

44
animals
sea animals

travel
sailing boat

other nouns
example

verbs
get undressed
have a swim
mean the same
pick up
take a bus
wait for a bus

**prepositional
phrases**
along the beach
by the sea

expressions
Be careful!
Quick!

45
other nouns
pirate
treasure

verbs
buy a ticket
climb trees
fall
go fishing
have something to
  eat

adjectives
awake
crazy
scary

pronouns
whose

46
transport
sail

clothes
a pair of glasses

verbs
catch a fish
dress up like a pirate
read about
swim in the sea

47
places
elevator
store

school
eraser

verbs
build
catch a train
drive a sports car
invite someone to a
  party
play garden games
laugh at funny films

travel to the moon
wait at the bus stop

48
verbs
make friends with
an alien
learn about
learn to swim
read e-books
read stories
ride on an elephant
sail round the world
go and see your
  grandparents
walk under a
waterfall
would like

sports and leisure
goal

49
home
clock

verbs
spell

expressions
Can you say that
  again?
How do you
  spell …?

50
school
English test
listening test
spelling test

leisure
football game
screen

Irregular verbs

Verb	Past simple	Translation
be	was/were	....
bring	brought	....
build	built	....
buy	bought	....
can	could	....
catch	caught	....
choose	chose	....
come	came	....
do	did	....
draw	drew	....
dream	dreamed/dreamt	....
drink	drank	....
drive	drove	....
eat	ate	....
fall	fell	....
find	found	....
fly	flew	....
get	got	....
give	gave	....
go	went	....
grow	grew	....
have	had	....
hide	hid	....
hit	hit	....
hold	held	....
hurt	hurt	....
know	knew	....

Verb	Past simple	Translation
learn	learned/learnt	....
lose	lost	....
make	made	....
mean	meant	....
put	put	....
read	read	....
ride	rode	....
run	ran	....
say	said	....
see	saw	....
send	sent	....
sing	sang	....
sit	sat	....
sleep	slept	....
spell	spelled/spelt	....
stand	stood	....
swim	swam	....
take	took	....
teach	taught	....
tell	told	....
think	thought	....
throw	threw	....
understand	understood	....
wake up	woke up	....
wear	wore	....
write	wrote	....